TERESA
of
AVILA

D0880623

TERESA
of
AVILA

The Way of Prayer

selected spiritual writings

introduced and edited by
Kieran Kavanaugh, O.C.D.

New City Press

Published in the United States by
New City Press, 202 Cardinal Rd., Hyde Park, NY 12538
www.newcitypress.com
© New City Press 2003

Front cover art, oil painting by Consuelo Bordas, Compagnia di Santa Teresa di Gesu.
Cover design by Nick Cianfarani

Library of Congress Cataloging-in-Publication Data:

Teresa, of Avila, Saint, 1515-1582.
    The way of prayer : selected spiritual writings / Teresa of Avila ; selected and
introduced by Kieran Kavanaugh.
        p. cm.
    Includes bibliographical references.
    ISBN 1-56548-181-X
    1. Prayer--Catholic Church. 2. Spiritual life--Catholic Church. I. Kavanaugh, Kieran,
    1928- II. Title.

BV215 .T38 2003
248--dc21   2002033710

Printed in Canada

Contents

Part 2
Glimmerings
from the Divine Depths

Abbreviations

All selections are from *The Collected Works of St. Teresa of Avila*, trans. Kieran Kavanaugh, O.C.D., and Otilio Rodriguez, O.C.D.., 3 vols. (Washington, D.C.: ICS Publications, 1976–85), or from *The Way of Perfection, A Study Edition* (Washington, D.C.: ICS Publications, 2000). The following abbreviations will be used in referring to Teresa's works:

F *The Book of Her Foundations* (vol. 3)

IC *The Interior Castle* (vol. 2)

L *The Book of Her Life* (vol. 1)

M *Meditations on the Song of Songs* (vol. 2)

ST *Spiritual Testimonies* (vol. 1)

W *The Way of Perfection* (vol. 2)

Introduction

Teresa's Early Years

Teresa de Ahumada was born to Alonso Sánchez de Cepeda and Beatriz de Ahumada on 28 March 1515 in the city of Avila, located on Spain's central plateau. To this day the city's walls are a vivid example of medieval fortification. As regards Teresa's roots, the attention in recent decades has focused on her father's early years in a *converso* family (Jews converted to Christianity). But the brief description of her father given by Teresa only shows him as a somewhat strict and devout Catholic. She was the fifth child in a family of three girls and nine boys. Two of the offspring were from Don Alonso's first wife who had died. In a society that favored rank, the family belonged to the class called *hidalgos*. We might describe this as belonging to the gentry rather than the nobility. Feeling the allurement of adventure and fortune all the boys eventually, and not surprisingly, set out for the newly discovered Americas.

Only thirteen when her mother died, with whom she had formed a close bond, Teresa began losing some of the fervor of her childhood. Her concerned father then decided to place her in the more restricted environment of a convent school conducted by Augustinian nuns. There she began to experience a call from God to become a nun, which she first resisted. But at the age of

twenty, she resolutely left home to enter the Carmelite Monastery of the Incarnation, even though having to leave her father
was heartbreaking for her. In her new home a much larger family
awaited her, one hundred fifty in all, from different classes in
society. And families in those times were much involved in the
life of a monastery, insisting that the nuns continue to hold the
rank they had in the world before entering.

Carmelite and Foundress

The Carmelite order traced its origins to hermits who lived on
Mount Carmel from the early thirteenth century. They had built
a chapel in the midst of their hermitages, dedicating it to Mary,
the Mother of Jesus. So Teresa often refers to the Carmelite order
as the Blessed Virgin's order. But the style of life at the Incarnation bore little resemblance to the life lived by the early hermits
in the Holy Land. It followed the patterns of Spanish communities for religious women. After two years, Teresa made her
profession of vows for life. But not much time passed before she
began to suffer from fever and fainting spells, a distressing and
serious illness that doctors were unable to diagnose. She finally
had to leave the monastery to seek a possible cure (through treat-
ment by a herbalist), which her father had arranged for her to
undergo as a last resort, but the regimen only worsened Teresa's
condition. Slipping into a coma lasting four days, she seemed to
many to be dead. Although she did survive the crisis, she
remained a paralytic for three years afterward and suffered the
rest of her life from deplorable health. But that she got better at
all, she attributed to the intercession of Saint Joseph to whom
she remained very devoted throughout her life. One of the
amazing features of her life was her ability to rise above her
illnesses and carry out her many and complicated affairs with
exceptional diligence and enthusiasm. It was sufficient for her
that she knew her endeavors were for the Lord's service.

The seriousness with which she undertook and persevered in
the practice of interior prayer, particularly after her father's

death in 1543, led ultimately as an effect of that prayer to her desire to live her religious life in a more perfect way. In 1562, supported by theologians, her confessor, and especially Saint Peter of Alcantara, she founded a small community in Avila that would consist of no more than fifteen nuns who wished to live together a life of prayer and solitude in the spirit of the primitive rule that was given to the hermits living on Mount Carmel by Saint Albert, patriarch of Jerusalem, at the beginning of the thirteenth century. Teresa's own spiritual graces and experience in prayer influenced as well the style of life she established in which all would be equal, of one rank, friends gathered around Christ who called them into his friendship. They would no longer cling to their family name, which could indicate a certain eminence, but take a religious title. From then on Teresa was known as Teresa of Jesus, but she is also frequently referred to as Teresa of Avila to distinguish her more clearly from other saints with the name Teresa. The new community would aim through prayer at serving the Church, the Body of Christ, suffering at the time serious threats against its unity. She thus gave an apostolic thrust to the pure contemplative life of her nuns. When the general of the Carmelite order, Giovanni Battista Rossi, visited Teresa's small community in Avila in 1567, he grew enthusiastic, encouraged her to set up more such communities, and gave her permission to found contemplative houses of friars as well. This marked the beginning of Teresa's persistent activity as a foundress. The friars lived a similar life but with the addition of a ministry of preaching and spiritual direction. These nuns and friars did not wear shoes, a symbol of their return to the primitive rule and a more contemplative manner of life. Popularly, they became known as discalced Carmelites.

Teresa's formidable task as foundress brought her into contact with people of all levels of society and walks of life. Passing into the pages of her life came a stream of bankers, muleteers, merchants, beggars, curates, theologians, bishops, dukes, duchesses, princes, and princesses—even the king, Philip II. Making every use of her charming gift for conversation and friendship, she was able to enlist generous support whenever there was need. She used to teach her nuns that "the holier you are the more sociable you will be."

When she began to hear reports coming from America of the millions who had not heard the gospel, she added prayer for the work of missionaries to the purpose of the contemplative life of her communities. This need made her even more zealous in her efforts to found new contemplative communities. She endured arduous travel through Castile and Andalusia in slow-moving covered wagons that never managed more than thirty miles a day. Sometimes she road on a donkey or a mule. A few times a wealthy friend provided her with a carriage for her journey, a more comfortable ride by far. In her travels, Teresa found a world that was nervous and tense. The Council of Trent had come and gone. The wars of religion had broken out again in France. In Spain the forces of the Inquisition were ominous. The unity of Christendom and Europe had broken and would stay broken.

Philip II, in his desire to keep Spain Catholic and in this way politically united, considered the reform of religious orders as one of many ways to achieve his goal. Consequently, he formed his own plans for the reform of religious orders. He appointed two Dominicans, Francisco Vargas and Pedro Fernández, as visitators of the Carmelite order. They had received powers to move religious from house to house and province to province, to assist superiors in their offices, and to depute other superiors from among either the Dominicans or the Carmelites. They were entitled to perform all acts necessary for the visitation, correction, and reform of both head and members of all houses of friars and nuns.

After she had founded eight of her new communities of nuns, Pedro Fernández ordered Teresa to return to the Incarnation as prioress and try to help that community, which had gotten bogged down under many financial and spiritual needs. She requested the young inspiring friar John of the Cross, whom she had recruited to initiate her new contemplative life among the male branch of the Carmelites, to assist her in the spiritual direction of the nuns at the Incarnation. In 1572 under his direction,

Teresa reached the highest stage of her journey in prayer, the spiritual marriage.

Subsequent to her successful years as prioress at the Incarnation, she made her first foundation in the southern part of Spain, in Beas de Segura in Andalusia. But that was also the year (1575) in which the general chapter of the Carmelite order was held in Piacenza, Italy. Seeking to confine the expansion of the discalced Carmelites in Spain and maintain control, the chapter took measures that led to serious jurisdictional conflicts between the king's desires for reform and the order's desire to hold on to its central authority. Teresa was caught in the middle. She wrote a number of letters trying to explain to the general the situation in Spain and the desire of the discalced friars and nuns to be loyal to him. But the letters, it seems, never reached him. The general needed to hear Teresa's explanation of what was happening in Spain and her avowals of loyalty and devotion. In the end, Teresa received orders from the chapter to choose one of her Castilian monasteries and confine herself to it. This kind of restriction was no cross for her. What saddened her was her inability to communicate with the general. In her letters, she assured him of her love, admiration, and prayers. Before receiving the command of Piacenza and returning to Castile to comply with it, she had made another foundation in Andalusia, this time in the famed city of Seville.

The chapter of Piacenza also issued orders that those who had been made superiors against the obedience due superiors within the order itself or had accepted offices or lived in monasteries or places prohibited by the same superiors should be removed. The monasteries of discalced friars in Andalusia were to be abandoned. These orders contradicted the commands issued by the apostolic visitators and the nuncio, Nicolò Ormaneto. But Ormaneto, who together with the king favored Teresa's work, died in 1577. When the new nuncio, Felippo Sega, arrived in Spain, he demonstrated a strong bias against Teresa and the discalced friars and nuns. He supported enforcement of the commands of the chapter of Piacenza, which led to the unjust arrest and imprisonment of John of the Cross in December of

1577. Later the nuncio placed the discalced friars and nuns under the jurisdiction of the provincials of Castile and Andalusia, and some of the leaders among the discalced friars were punished and restricted to one monastery. During the troublesome years after the chapter of Piacenza, Teresa's project seemed to be crumbling. Nonetheless, she did not always agree with the actions of her discalced friars and had to admit the disturbing indiscretion of some of their actions.

In the midst of these persecutions, Teresa always felt a strong trust in God and a conviction that in the end her work would go undestroyed. Furthermore, nothing could prevent her from entering the innermost room of her soul where she enjoyed the tranquil presence of the Holy Trinity. With her exceptional talent for cooling tempers and enlisting support for her ideals, she could have undoubtedly appeased the members of the chapter of Piacenza had she been there to speak to them. That not being the case, she turned to letter writing, which came to play an essential role in her work as foundress. Once she claimed that the biggest burden of her whole effort as foundress was her correspondence. It is estimated that she wrote up to fifteen thousand letters, and some calculations go as high as twenty-five thousand. But only about 450 of these have survived. She seized every moment she could to work at this task. In the time of crisis, then, after Sega's arrival, she carried on a campaign in favor of her friars and nuns, writing to as many influential people as she could think of. Letters went to Rome, the king, bishops, people of the nobility, to anyone she thought could help.

In the end, through the intervention of the king, in 1580, the discalced Carmelites received permission to form a separate province. The previous year Teresa was allowed to take up her travels again. Travel for Teresa, with her miserable health, had often been a veritable torment. In those days, even if in excellent health, few found anything pleasurable about it. Making three more foundations before her last one in Burgos in 1582, Teresa ended with a total of seventeen monasteries of her nuns, all of which are still in existence. After making the foundation in Burgos, worn out from years of poor health, overwork, and conflict, she set off in return to Avila. On the way, in obedience to her provincial, she was obliged to renounce her plans and stop in Alba de Tormes because of a request made to the provincial by the Duchess of Alba. She arrived at her monastery in Alba seriously ill. Within a fortnight, on 4 October 1582, after ardent impulses of love expressed on the previous day, she died quietly and peacefully, between nine and ten in the evening.

Her Spiritual Journey

Since the selections for this anthology deal mainly with Teresa's interior experience and teachings on prayer, a further word is needed to point out some of the salient dates and facts surrounding Teresa's interior life and development. These will provide us with a generic framework to aid in the understanding of the passages included in this book. In Teresa's life, prayer and its process coincide with the unfolding of her spiritual journey. Also, as a prominent aspect of her life of prayer, contemplation coincides with mystical life. She calls infused contemplation "supernatural contemplation," understanding by the term the entire gamut of forms and degrees of passive, infused, mystical prayer. These stages or degrees of contemplation result from her own inner life and are well known by students of Christian spirituality.

At the center of Teresa's life story lies her conversion experience of 1554, which occurred when she was thirty-nine after she had lived about nineteen years as a nun in the Carmelite Monastery of the Incarnation. Her spiritual life before her conversion was marked by intense ascetical struggle; the life that followed was clearly mystical consisting in a continual ascent of increasing intensity amid a superabundance of gifts. The first stage, even before her entry into a monastery of nuns, lacked unity and continuity. It followed an undulating, winding path with highs and lows and notable breakdowns.

One way of presenting her life is to separate it into three periods. The first would cover her childhood and youth up to her entry into religious life (1515–1535). The second would include her initial years as a Carmelite nun. This would comprise her serious painful illness; her return to prayer after her father's death; and the faint beginnings of her mystical life leading to her conversion in 1554. The third stage then follows in a continuous line the steps recounted in the fifth, sixth, and seventh dwelling places of her *Interior Castle*, a work reputed to be the best version of Teresa's spiritual biography.

In her childhood readings of the lives of the saints, among the many unconnected and extraordinary episodes reported, Teresa began to focus on the value of the eternal next to the passing character of all things temporal. She grasped this and expressed it in a kind of mantra she loved to repeat over and over and that for us evokes thoughts of the Book of Revelations (22:5) or even Handel's Messiah: "forever and ever and ever." Her heart was next moved and stirred to action, to go off to the land of the Moors, not out of missionary zeal but to suffer martyrdom and win heaven quickly. Heaven, after all, is the highest aim of contemplatives. This fervent desire accounted in part for a tension that continued throughout her life between the church on earth and the church in heaven. Biographers of our times would easily file this story of Teresa's ardor for martyrdom in her childhood under the category of legend had she not left us her own report of her attempt to leave home to have her head cut off for being a Christian.

When this attempt was blocked by her parents after a frantic search, she turned to an ingenuous attempt at the life of a solitary by imitating the early hermits in a corner of her garden. It seems she was already feeling the first hint of a call to contemplation.

Later on, after a crisis in her youth in which she slipped from her early fervor, she gradually turned back to the ideals of her childhood and felt drawn to a better life. This came about particularly through the good influence and friendship of an Augustinian nun at the convent school in which her father had arranged for her to live.

Books once more inspired her. While reading *The Letters of Saint Jerome*, she felt strongly the urge to stop resisting a call to be a nun. Later after entering the monastery of the Incarnation in Avila, she was deeply impressed by reading Francisco de Osuna's *Third Spiritual Alphabet* and Saint Gregory the Great's *Morals on Job*. From her acquaintance with Job in the latter book she discovered a model that lay at the root of her own idea of prayer and her own personal method of practicing it. From Osuna's book she learned about the prayer of recollection. The book spoke to the profound contemplative call within her and helped her take the first needed steps along the way of a response.

We know comparatively little about the prayer of her earlier years, but we do know that she liked to represent Christ within her and especially in those scenes from his life where she saw him more alone. Previous to her own mystical experience, she lacked any kind of theoretical knowledge about the mystical life and was completely surprised when she began to receive a more habitual infusion of contemplative graces.

As for the initial appearances of her contemplation, Teresa has left sufficient information. In the second stage mentioned above (1535–1544), her journey winds its way through intermittent waves of recollection and quiet and even some moments of union. These served to increase her desire for prayer in solitude. Also during this period she had an unusual vision, fleeting and without effect, of Christ looking severely at her while she was visiting with a gentleman in the parlor. In some way the extraordinary graces that were to come, described in her *Life* and *Interior Castle*, were being briefly anticipated. Although from the picture Teresa paints for us of herself we have reason to suspect that during this period some contemplative graces were granted to her, they were ordinarily absent from her life.

Noticeable in this stage is what we might call a period of transition that began with the death of her father, Don Alonso, until her definitive conversion. It consists of ten years between two conversions, and for her to be converted involved prayer. In 1544, Teresa decided to return to her daily practice of prayer after having abandoned it for about a year or so. Ten years later she underwent a radical and total conversion that brought her to the point of complete submission to all the exigencies of contemplation. During those ten years, Teresa suffered through a veritable struggle between her prayer life and all that warred against it. As she worded it, the conflict was between friendship with God and friendship with the world.

In the midst of this struggle she began to perceive the faint signs of passive prayer in the form of what is called initial contemplation, a contemplation which though not "perfect" or "pure" is nonetheless "supernatural" or "mystical." Although this grace was sporadic, it tended to recur, summoning Teresa to a more intense spiritual life until she reached the point of a definitive change.

When Teresa translated this period of her experience into theory, she placed it in the fourth dwelling place of her *Interior Castle,* a setting in which the Teresian natural and supernatural are interwoven in experiences of recollection and quiet. These first glimmerings of contemplation were tenuous, accounting for the frequent occurrences of difficulty in prayer and a need for ascetical struggle.

With Teresa's conversion in 1554, contemplative prayer, the prayer of quiet and often of union, became habitual and would last a long while. Contemplation began to pervade her life. She classifies this period as the fifth dwelling place in which the initial stage of union presents itself. Later during these years (1554–60), she also heard the Lord speak to her for the first time. Her prayer as an intimate sharing between friends reached a fulness of reality in which her divine Lord began perceptibly taking part in the conversation.

Her first rapture produced the effect of a noticeable progress in the sense that contemplation is a communion or friendship with God alone which extends to the whole of life. Her first vision initiated a kind of sharing or communion or communication that was purely contemplative and prolonged, in the form of an intellectual gaze and a silent mutual presence between Teresa and her Lord.

In the second and third phases of her mystical life (1560–72 and 1572–82), which correspond to her descriptions in the sixth and seventh dwelling places of *The Interior Castle*, her contemplative life increased in intensity with a multiplicity of forms. A continuity, however, is revealed through a threefold line of development. We find the sharing (locutions), the visual contemplation (visions, intellectual and imaginative, of the humanity of Christ which culminate in the intellectual visions of the Godhead and the Holy Trinity), and ultimately the divine presence. In the last decade of her life, amid a bluster of activities and obligations, Teresa felt drawn continually into the warm orbit of deep intimate communion with the Holy Trinity. This became her contemplative mode of living (1572–1582).

In her *Life,* writing for her spiritual guides about her ultimate contemplative experiences, she found herself actually in what she later termed the sixth dwelling place. About ten years later, at the time she was composing her *Interior Castle* and describing the sixth and seventh dwelling places, she was working from out of a horizon that had undergone a fundamental change. The grace of spiritual marriage, its ever-present depth of peace, had been her spiritual patrimony for some years. This supreme abiding peace contrasted with the spiritual impulses and fervent longings of ecstatic love and desire for death that were present as she brought *The Book of Her Life* to a close. This interior quiet and calm remained until the end of her earthly life, a fact that stands out clearly in the final account of her spiritual life written for her director at the end of her life.

Her Writings

The many favors Teresa received from God in prayer were not without their purpose. The effort to explain her interior life led to the writing of her books, some of which I have already referred to in passing. Her first large endeavor, *The Book of Her Life*, its final form was completed in 1565. Here she tells the story of her early years, of God's graces and her failures, and about her vocation. After a small treatise on prayer inserted into the middle of her story to prepare the reader for the comprehension of what was to occur next, she takes up again her account, dwelling especially on the mystical path which worked strikingly beneficial changes in her. The last chapters tell the story of the heavy opposition she encountered when making her first foundation in Avila.

In the small treatise she compares her growth in prayer to four ways in which gardens were watered in her day. The first way of watering the garden entails a good deal of human activity. The other ways point to a gradual lessening of activity and an increase of passivity until, in the fourth, an abundant rain pours down freely. She often abbreviates her references to these degrees of prayer by simply calling them "waters," the first water, the second water, and so on. The graces of the fourth water played their role in her initiatives to found her first little community. They were graces of union, which she divides into simple and ecstatic union. The ecstatic union was at times accompanied by locutions, visions, and revelations.

The Way of Perfection was completed in its revised form by about 1567. In this work she describes the main virtues that are necessary for the contemplative way of life she had established. But the virtues explained are the practices of charity, detachment, and humility, virtues appropriate for all disciples of Christ. She then presents a masterful commentary on the Our Father, which provided her with the opportunity to explain the path of prayer, which leads to contemplation, to Christ, the fount of living waters.

The Meditations on the Song of Songs, of uncertain date, is a small but doctrinally rich reflection on some verses from the biblical text *The Song of Songs*.

The Interior Castle, written in 1577, giving a complete picture of the journey in prayer, is based on the evolution of Teresa's own inner experience. The development unfolds through an inward movement that traverses many rooms set up into seven categories. They lead to the center, the seventh dwelling place, where the Holy Trinity abides. The light from the center room attracting the soul inward reaches out in lesser or greater degree to the other dwelling places according to their distance from the center. One enters the castle through prayer. As the journey inward through the dwelling places progresses, the prayer, as with the ways of watering the garden, becomes increasingly passive; that is, received as a gift from God whose presence is lovingly and secretly made known. But in speaking of seven dwelling places, Teresa meant to suggest bountifulness and variety. In each category are many other dwelling places with lovely gardens and fountains. In the seventh dwelling place, a new world opens before us that had not yet been revealed to Teresa when she wrote her first book. This compelling work has received wide acclaim as Teresa's masterpiece.

The Spiritual Testimonies consist of a collection of short reports of her spiritual experiences. They were written down in the course of the last two decades of her life.

In *The Book of Her Foundations*, which was begun in 1573 and continues up through her last foundation in 1582, the final year of her life, Teresa describes the complex events surrounding her laborious and untiring work as foundress. In this book we read of the tangled situations and painful misunderstandings that gave scope to her exceptional human qualities and talents. These gifts continue to attract many to her spirit. But she always insisted that her new communities were the work of God.

The Content of Her Contemplation

The Teresian writings present to the theologian a copious store of contemplative experiences having for their object the Christian mysteries. Offered in simple form without literary adornment or artificial garb, these experiences are freed of outlines or systems of thought, nor are they filtered through the sieve of philosophical or theological frameworks and categories. In this unprocessed material, Teresa is at once both witness and actor. She gives witness with an unsparing care to be truthful and accurate and frank. This required a special effort because the experiences themselves lie beyond the pale of words. When she does use some technical terms, philosophical, psychological, or theological, she does so precariously, fully aware of her limitations but eager to use any means that might help her explain.

In studying this virgin material, scholars have usually explored the development of the prayer life and the experiences of Teresa as recipient of contemplation: quiet, union, ecstasy, and so on. Or they have focused on the psychic zones, the senses, faculties and their activities, and the depth of the soul. Much less attention has been paid to the objective element, the objects contemplated, the mysteries of the divine world that Teresa encountered in her contemplation. In this sphere she offers us rich material. Hardly a sector of the Christian revelation is missing from her contemplative graces.

Teresa, then, like other prophets, saints, doctors, and mystics may serve as a prism to show the divine light in a marvelous variety of colors. She becomes a splendid tool for investigating the sacred mysteries and arriving at the profundities of Christ's love, "which surpasses all knowledge" (Eph. 19:3). The objective content of her contemplation has the power to snatch us up as well into the intimacy of knowledge and love that she experienced in the divine mysteries. With this help from her, the Holy Spirit may touch us as well and make us sharers in that blessed communion.

The first section of this anthology will center on texts suggesting Teresa's own growth in the spiritual life, particularly in her life of prayer. Then as Teresa moved into the world of contemplation, she began to receive deep illuminations concerning the mysteries of the Christian faith. The theologian might easily enough divide these into categories, such as christological, trinitarian, and soteriological.

As a result the texts gathered in the second section of this anthology are worthy of more than a quick reading and are no less important than those in the first. The objective content of Teresa's contemplation can take hold of us and lead us into deep abysses, where we can catch some glimmerings of God's mysteries that no theologian or spiritual writer may have succeeded in bringing into our awareness. The objects of her contemplation as Teresa falteringly describes them surprise us by their power and theological profundity, highlighting the eloquent truth that God who is Love is only attained through love. In the words of John, "Love is of God; everyone who loves is begotten of God and has knowledge of God" (1 Jn. 4:7).

When saints embrace the mystery of God with the totality of their being, and love the Lord with all their hearts, they include their neighbor. The practice of the love of the Lord in prayer will weaken and become effete without the practice of the love of neighbor. The Holy Spirit brought the two together in Teresa in a beautiful counterpoint: love of our neighbor, who is visible; love of God who is invisible. The good she was destined to bring to her neighbor was the way of prayer, the good she grew to cherish.

Teresa always extols the extraordinary mystical favors lavishly bestowed on her by God and especially their fruits. She protests against any who would tend to depreciate such graces. At the same time she adamantly insisted that these favors can never be elicited through studied techniques, and warned her readers not to expect or desire them, that they are not required for sanctity. She states her view clearly in her *Foundations*:

> The highest perfection obviously does not consist in interior delights or in great raptures or in visions or in the spirit of prophecy but in having our will so much in conformity with God's will that there is nothing we know he wills that we do not want with all our desire, and in accepting the bitter as happily as we do the delightful when we know that His Majesty desires it. This seems most difficult (not the doing of it, but this being content with what completely contradicts our nature); and indeed it truly is difficult. But love has this strength if it is perfect, for we forget about pleasing ourselves in order to please the one we love. And truly this is so; for even though the trials may be very great, they become sweet when we know we are pleasing God. And this is the way by which those who have reached this stage love persecutions, dishonor, and offenses. This is so certain, so well known, and so plain that there is no reason for me to delay over the matter (F. 5.7).

Part 1

A Story of Prayer

Chapter 1

A Call From God:
Childhood, Youth, Severe Illness

My brothers and sisters did not in any way hold me back from the service of God. I had one brother about my age. We used to get together to read the lives of the saints. (He was the one I liked most, although I had great love for them all and they for me.) When I considered the martyrdoms the saints suffered for God, it seemed to me that the price they paid for going to enjoy God was very cheap, and I greatly desired to die in the same way. I did not want this on account of the love I felt for God but to get to enjoy very quickly the wonderful things I read there were in heaven. And my brother and I discussed together the means we should take to achieve this. We agreed to go off to the land of the Moors and beg them, out of love of God, to cut off our heads there. It seemed to me the Lord had given us courage at so tender an age, but we couldn't discover any means. Having parents seemed to us the greatest obstacle. We were terrified in what we read about the suffering and the glory that was to last forever. We spent a lot of time talking about this and took delight in often repeating: forever and ever and ever. As I said this over and over, the Lord was pleased to impress upon me in childhood the way of truth.

When I saw it was impossible to go where I would be killed for God, we made plans to be hermits. And in a garden that we had in our house, we tried as we could to make hermitages piling up some little stones which afterwards would quickly fall down again. And so in nothing could we find a remedy for our desire. It gives me devotion now to see how God gave me so early what I lost through my own fault.

I gave what alms I could, but that was little. I sought out solitude to pray my devotions, and they were many, especially the rosary, to which my mother was very devoted; and she made us devoted to it too. When I played with other girls I enjoyed it when we pretended we were nuns in a monastery, and it seemed to me that I desired to be one (L. 1.4–6).

Beginning, then, to like the good and holy conversation of this nun, I was glad to hear how well she spoke about God, for she was very discreet and saintly. There was no time it seems to me when I was not happy to hear about God. She began to tell me how she arrived at the decision to become a nun solely by reading what the Gospel says: "many are the called and few the chosen" [Mt. 22:14]. She told me about the reward the Lord grants those who give up all for him. This good company began to help me get rid of the habits that the bad company had caused and to turn my mind to the desire for eternal things and for some freedom from the antagonism that I felt strongly within myself toward becoming a nun (L. 3.1).

My fondness for good books was my salvation. Reading the Letters of Saint Jerome so encouraged me that I decided to tell my father about my decision to take the habit, for I was so persistent in points of honor that I don't think I would have turned back for anything once I told him (L. 3.7).

As soon as I took the habit, the Lord gave me an understanding of how he favors those who use force with themselves to serve him. No one noticed this struggle, but rather they thought that I was very pleased. Within an hour, he gave me such great happiness at being in the religious state of life that it never left me up to this day, and God changed the dryness my soul experienced into the greatest tenderness. All the things of religious life delighted me, and it is true that sometimes while sweeping, during the hours I used to spend in self-indulgence and self-adornment, I realized that I was free of all that and experienced a new joy which amazed me. And I could not understand where it came from (L. 4.2).

The cure was supposed to begin at the beginning of the summer, and I went at the beginning of the winter. During that interval I stayed, waiting for the month of April, at my sister's house, which I mentioned, which was in a hamlet nearby; and I didn't have to be coming and going.

When I was on the way, that uncle of mine I mentioned who lived along the road gave me a book. It is called *The Third Spiritual Alphabet* [by Francisco de Osuna] and endeavors to teach the prayer of recollection. And although during this first year I read good books (for I no longer desired to make use of the others, because I understood the harm they did me), I did not know how to proceed in prayer or how to be recollected. And so I was very happy with this book and resolved to follow that path with all my strength. Since the Lord had already given me the gift of tears and I enjoyed reading, I began to take time out for solitude, to confess frequently, and to follow that path, taking the book for my master. For during the twenty years after this period of which I am speaking, I did not find a master, I mean a confessor, who understood me, even though I looked for one. This hurt me so much that I often turned back and was even completely lost, for a master would have helped me flee from the occasions of offending God.

His Majesty began to grant me many favors during these early stages. I was almost nine months in this solitude, although not so free from offending God as the book told me I should be; but I could not be that free, for it seemed to me almost impossible to be so on guard. I kept from committing mortal sin and begged God to keep me so always. As for venial sins, I paid little attention; and that is what destroyed me. At the end of this time that I mentioned there, the Lord, as I was saying, began to favor me by means of this path; so much so that he granted me the prayer of quiet. And sometimes I arrived at union, although I did not understand what the one was or the other, or how much they were to be prized—for I believe it would have done me great good to have understood this. True, this union lasted for so short a time that I do not know if it continued for the space of a Hail Mary. But I was left with some effects so great that, even though at this time I was no more than twenty, it seems I trampled the world under foot. And so I pitied those who went following after it, even though in permissible things.

I tried as hard as I could to keep Jesus Christ, our God and our Lord, present within me, and that was my way of prayer. If I reflected upon some phase of his passion, I represented him to myself interiorly. But most of the time I spent reading good books, which was my whole recreation. For God didn't give me talent for discursive thought or for a profitable use of the imagination. In fact, my imagination is so dull that I never succeeded even to think about and represent in my mind—as hard as I tried—the humanity of the Lord. And although, if one perseveres, one reaches contemplation more quickly along this way of inability to work discursively with the intellect, this way is nonetheless most laborious and painful. For if the will is not occupied and love has nothing present with which to be engaged, the soul is left as though without support or exercise, and the solitude and dryness is very troublesome, and the battle with one's thoughts extraordinary (L. 4.6–7).

Seeing such poor results, my father brought me back to where doctors could come to see me. They all gave up hope for me, for they said that on top of all this sickness, I was also tubercular. I cared little about this diagnosis. The pains were what exhausted me, for they were like one continuous entity throughout my whole body, from head to foot. Pain of the nerves is unbearable, as doctors affirm, and since my nerves were all shrunken, certainly it was a bitter torment. How many merits could I have gained, were it not for my own fault!

I remained in this excruciating state no more than three months, for it seemed impossible to be able to suffer so many ills together. Now I am amazed; and I consider the patience His Majesty gave me a great favor from the Lord, for this patience was clearly seen to come from him. It greatly profited me to have read the story of Job in Saint Gregory's *Morals*. For it seems the Lord prepared me by this means, together with my having begun to experience prayer, so that I could be able to bear the suffering with so much conformity to his will. All my conversations were with him. I kept these words of Job very habitually in my mind and recited them: "Since we receive good things from the hand of the Lord, why do we not suffer the evil things?" [Jb. 2:10]. This it seems gave me strength (L. 5.8).

Right away I was in such a hurry to return to the convent that I made them bring me back as I was. The one they expected to be brought back dead they received alive; but the body, worse than dead, was a pity to behold. The state of my weakness was indescribable, for I was then only bones. I may add that the above condition lasted for more than eight months. The paralysis, although it gradually got better, lasted almost three years. When I began to go about on hands and knees, I praised God. With great conformity to his will, I suffered all those years and—if not in these early sufferings—with great gladness. For it was all a trifle to me in comparison with the pains and torments suffered in the beginning. I was very conformed to the will of God, and I would have remained so even had he left me in this condition forever. It seems to me that all my longing to be cured was that I might remain alone in prayer as was my custom, for in the infirmary the suitable means for this was lacking. I went to confession very often. I spoke much about God in such a way that I was edifying to everyone, and they were amazed at the patience the Lord gave me. For if this patience had not come from the hand of His Majesty, it seemed it would have been impossible to suffer so much with so great contentment.

It was a great thing that he had granted me the favor in prayer which he did, for this made me understand the meaning of love of him. For within that short time I saw some new virtues arise in me (although they were not strong since they were insufficient to sustain me in righteousness): not speaking evil of anyone, no matter how slight, but ordinarily avoiding all fault-finding. I was very much aware that I should not desire to say of another person what I would not want him to say of me (L. 6.2–3).

Chapter 2

Struggles along the Path of Prayer

There remained in me the desire for solitude and a fondness for conversing and speaking about God. If I found someone with whom to speak thus, it gave me more happiness and recreation than all the suave—coarse, to use a better word—conversation of the world. I received Communion and confessed much more often and desired to do so. I liked to read good books very much, and felt the deepest repentance after having offended God. For often, I recall, I did not dare pray, because I feared as I would a severe punishment the very bitter sorrow I would have to feel at having offended God. This went on increasing afterward to such an extreme that I don't know what to compare the torment to. This feeling did not in any way spring from fear, but since I remembered the favors the Lord granted me in prayer and the many things I owed him, and I saw how badly I was repaying him, I could not endure it. And seeing my lack of amendment, I became extremely vexed about the many tears I was shedding over my faults, for neither were my resolutions nor were the hardships I suffered enough to keep me from placing myself in the occasion and falling again. They seemed fraudulent tears to me, and afterward the fault appeared to be greater, because I saw the wonderful favor the Lord bestowed in giving me these tears and such deep repentance. I endeavored to go to confession right away and, in my opinion, I did what I could to return to God's grace.

The whole trouble lay in not getting at the root of the occasions and with my confessors who were of little help. For had they told me of the danger I was in and that I had the obligation to avoid those friendships, without a doubt I believe I would have remedied the matter. For in no way would I have endured being in mortal sin even for a day should I have understood that to be the case.

All these signs of fear of God came to me during prayer; and the greatest sign was that they were enveloped in love, for punishment did not enter my mind. This carefulness of conscience with respect to mortal sin lasted all during my illness. Oh, God help me, how I desired my health so as to serve him more, and this health was the cause of all my harm (L. 6.4).

Since I thus began to go from pastime to pastime, from vanity to vanity, from one occasion to another, to place myself so often in very serious occasions, and to allow my soul to become so spoiled by many vanities, I was then ashamed to return to the search for God by means of a friendship as special as is that found in the intimate exchange of prayer. And I was aided in this vanity by the fact that as the sins increased I began to lose joy in virtuous things and my taste for them. I saw very clearly, my Lord, that these were failing me because I was failing you (L. 7.1).

When I was sick during those first days before I knew how to take care of myself, I had the greatest desire to help others improve, a very common temptation of beginners, although in my case it turned out well. Since I loved my father so much, I desired for him the good I felt I got out of the practice of prayer. It seemed to me that in this life there could be no greater good than the practice of prayer. So in roundabout ways, as much as I could, I began to strive to get him to pray. I gave him books for this purpose. Since he had such virtue, as I mentioned, he settled into this practice so well that within five or six years—it seems it was—he was so advanced that I praised the Lord very much, and it gave me the greatest consolation. Very severe were the many kinds of trials he had; all of them he suffered with the deepest conformity to God's will. He came often to see me, for it consoled him to speak of the things of God.

After I had begun to live in such havoc, and without practicing prayer, and since I saw that he thought I was living as usual, I could not bear to let him be deceived. For thinking it was the more humble thing to do, I had gone a year and more without prayer. And this, as I shall say afterward, was the greatest temptation I had, because on account of this I was heading just about straight to perdition. For when I practiced prayer, I offended God one day but then others I turned to recollection and withdrew more from the occasions.

Since this blessed man came to talk with me about prayer, it was a bitter thing for me to see him so deceived as to think I conversed with God as I was accustomed before. And I told him that I no longer practiced prayer, but didn't give the reason. I brought up my illnesses as making it impossible for me (L. 7.10–11).

But this was not sufficient cause to set aside something for which bodily strength is not necessary but only love and a habit; and the Lord always provides the opportunity if we desire. I say "always" because although on occasion and also sometimes in sickness we are impeded from having hours free for solitude, there is no lack of other time when we have the health for this. And even in sickness itself and these other occasions the prayer is genuine when it comes from a soul that loves to offer the sickness up and accept what is happening and be conformed to it and to the other thousand things that happen. Prayer is an exercise of love, and it would be incorrect to think that if there is no time for solitude there is no prayer at all. With a little care great blessings can come when because of our labors the Lord takes from us the time we had set for prayer. And so I have found these blessings when I have had a good conscience (L 7.12).

For in order to resemble in some way a father like this I should have improved. His confessor—who was a Dominican, a very learned man—said he did not doubt but that my father had gone straight to heaven. He had been confessor to my father for some years and praised his purity of conscience.

This Dominican father, who was very good and God-fearing, profited me a great deal. For I went to confession to him, and he took it upon himself with care to do good for my soul and make me understand the perdition that I was bringing on myself. He had me receive Communion every fifteen days. And, little by little, in beginning to talk to him, I discussed my prayer with him. He told me not to let it go, that it could in no way do me anything but good. I began to return to it, although not to give up the occasions of sin; and I never again abandoned it.

I was living an extremely burdensome life, because in prayer I understand more clearly my faults. On the one hand God was calling me; on the other hand I was following the world. All the things of God made me happy; those of the world held me bound. It seems I desired to harmonize these two contraries—so inimical to one another—such as are the spiritual life and sensory joys, pleasures, and pastimes. In prayer I was having great trouble, for my spirit was not proceeding as lord but as slave. And so I was not able to shut myself within myself (which was my whole manner of procedure in prayer); instead, I shut within myself a thousand vanities.

Thus I passed many years, for now I am surprised how I could have put up with both and not abandon either the one or the other. Well do I know that to abandon prayer was no longer in my hands, for he held me in his, he who desired to give me greater favors (L. 7.16–17).

For this reason I would counsel those who practice prayer to seek, at least in the beginning, friendship and association with other persons having the same interest. This is something most important even though the association may be only to help one another with prayers. The more of these prayers there are, the greater the gain. Since friends are sought out for conversations and human attachments, even though these latter may not be good, so as to relax and better enjoy telling about vain pleasures, I don't know why it is not permitted that persons beginning truly to love and to serve God talk with some others about their joys and trials, which all who practice prayer undergo. For if the friendship they desired to have with His Majesty is authentic, there is no reason to fear vainglory. And when these persons overcome vainglory in its first stirrings, they come away with merit. I believe that they who discuss these joys and trials for the sake of this friendship with God will benefit themselves and those who hear them, and they will come away instructed; even without understanding how they will have instructed their friends (L. 7.20).

I should say that it is one of the most painful lives, I think, that one can imagine; for neither did I enjoy God nor did I find happiness in the world. When I was experiencing the enjoyments of the world, I felt sorrow when I recalled what I owed to God. When I was with God, my attachments to the world disturbed me. This is a war so troublesome that I don't know how I was able to suffer it even a month, much less for so many years.

However, I see clearly the great mercy the Lord bestowed on me; for though I continued to associate with the world, I had the courage to practice prayer. I say courage, for I do not know what would require greater courage among all the things there are in the world than to betray the king and know that he knows it and yet never leave his presence. Though we are always in the presence of God, it seems to me the manner is different with those who practice prayer, for they are aware that he is looking at them. With others, it can happen that several days pass without their recalling that God sees them.

True, during these years there were many months, and I believe sometimes a year, that I kept from offending the Lord. And I put forth some effort, and at times a great deal of it, not to offend him. Because all that I write is said with complete truthfulness, I shall treat of this effort now. But I remember little of these good days, and so they must have been few; and a lot about the bad ones. Few days passed without my devoting long periods to prayer, unless I was very sick or very busy. When I was sick, I felt better when with God. I tried to get persons who talked with me to practice prayer, and I besought the Lord for them. I frequently spoke of him.

So, save for the year I mentioned, for more than eighteen of the twenty-eight years since I began prayer, I suffered this battle and conflict between friendship with God and friendship with the world. During the remaining years of which I have yet to speak, the cause of the war changed, although the war was not a small one. But since it was, in my opinion, for the service of God and with knowledge of the vanity that the world is, everything went smoothly, as I shall say afterward.

I have recounted all this at length, as I already mentioned, so that the mercy of God and my ingratitude might be seen; also, in order that one might understand the great good God does for a soul that willingly disposes itself for the practice of prayer, even though it is not as disposed as is necessary. I recount this also that one may understand how if the soul perseveres in prayer, in the midst of the sins, temptations, and failures of a thousand kinds that the devil places in its path, in the end, I hold as certain, the Lord will draw it forth to the harbor of salvation as—now it seems—he did for me. May it please His Majesty that I do not get lost again (L. 8.2–5).

But I must have failed, as it appears to me now, because I did not put all my trust in His Majesty and lose completely the trust I had in myself. I searched for a remedy, I made attempts, but I didn't understand that all is of little benefit if we do not take away completely the trust we have in ourselves and place it in God (L. 8.12).

Well, my soul now was tired; and, in spite of its desire, my wretched habits would not allow it rest. It happened to me that one day entering the oratory I saw a statue they had borrowed for a certain feast to be celebrated in the house. It represented the much wounded Christ and was very devotional so that beholding it I was utterly distressed in seeing him that way, for it well represented what he suffered for us. I felt so keenly aware of how poorly I thanked him for those wounds that, it seems to me, my heart broke. Beseeching him to strengthen me once and for all that I might not offend him, I threw myself down before him with the greatest outpouring of tears.

I was very devoted to the glorious Magdalene and frequently thought about her conversion, especially when I received Communion. For since I knew the Lord was certainly present there within me, I, thinking that he would not despise my tears, placed myself at his feet. And I don't know what I was saying (he did a great deal who allowed me to shed them for him, since I so quickly forgot that sentiment); and I commended myself to this glorious saint that she might obtain pardon for me.

But in this latter instance with this statue I am speaking of, it seems to me I profited more, for I was very distrustful of myself and placed all my trust in God. I think I then said that I would not rise from there until he granted what I was begging him for. I believe certainly this was beneficial to me, because from that time I went on improving (L. 9.1–3).

Chapter 3

General Teachings on the Way of Prayer

Now returning to those who want to journey on this road and continue until they reach the end, which is to drink from this water of life [Jn. 4:14], I say that how they are to begin is very important—in fact, all important. They must have a great and very determined determination to persevere until reaching the end, come what may, happen what may, whatever work is involved, whatever criticism arises, whether they arrive or whether they die on the road, or even if they don't have courage for the trials that are met, or if the whole world collapses (W. 21.2).

Before I say anything about interior matters, that is, about prayer, I shall mention some things that are necessary for those who seek to follow the way of prayer; so necessary that even if these persons are not very contemplative, they can be far advanced in the service of the Lord if they possess these things. And if they do not possess them, it is impossible for them to be very contemplative. And if they think they are, they are being highly deceived. May the Lord help me speak of these things, and may he teach me what I am about to say so that it may be for his glory, amen.

Do not think, my friends and daughters, that I shall burden you with many things; please God, we shall do what our holy fathers established and observed, for by walking this path they themselves established they merited this title we give them. It would be wrong to seek another way or try to learn about this path from anyone else. I shall enlarge on only three things, which are from our own constitutions, for it is very important that we understand how much the practice of these three things helps us to possess inwardly and outwardly the peace our Lord recommended so highly to us. The first of these is love for one another; the second is detachment from all created things; the third is true humility, which, even though I speak of it last, is the main practice and embraces all the others.

About the first, love for one another, it is most important that we have this, for there is nothing annoying that is not suffered easily by those who love one another—a thing would have to be extremely annoying before causing any displeasure. And if this commandment were observed in the world as it should be, I think such love would be very helpful for the observance of the other commandments (W. 4.4–5).

A great aid to going against your will is to bear in mind continually how all is vanity and how quickly everything comes to an end. This helps to remove our attachment to trivia and center it on what will never end. Even though this practice seems to be a weak means, it will strengthen the soul greatly, and the soul will be most careful in very little things. When we begin to become attached to something, we should strive to turn our thoughts from it and bring them back to God—and His Majesty helps. He has done us a great favor because in this house most of the work of detachment has been done—although this turning and being against ourselves is a difficult thing because we live very close together and love ourselves greatly.

Here true humility can enter the picture because this virtue and the virtue of detachment it seems to me always go together. They are two inseparable sisters. These are not the relatives I advise you to withdraw from; rather, you should embrace them and love them and never be seen without them. O sovereign virtues, rulers over all creation, emperors of the world, deliverers from all snares and entanglements laid by the devil, virtues so loved by our teacher Christ who never for a moment was seen without them! Those who have them can easily go out and fight with all hell together and against the whole world and all its occasions of sin. Such persons have no fear of anyone, for theirs is the kingdom of heaven. They have no one to fear because they don't care if they lose everything, nor would they consider this a loss. The only thing they fear is displeasing their God, and they beg God to sustain them in these virtues lest they lose them through their own fault (W. 10.2–3).

Mental Prayer

Whoever has not begun the practice of prayer, I beg for the love of the Lord not to go without so great a good. There is nothing here to fear but only something to desire. Even if there be no great progress, or much effort in reaching such perfection as to deserve the favors and mercies God bestows on the more generous, at least a person will come to understand the road leading to heaven. And if one perseveres, I trust then in the mercy of God, who never fails to repay anyone who has taken him for a friend. For mental prayer in my opinion is nothing else than an intimate sharing between friends; it means taking time frequently to be alone with him who we know loves us. In order that love be true and the friendship endure, the wills of the friends must be in accord. The will of the Lord, it is already known, cannot be at fault; our will is vicious, sensual, and ungrateful. And if you do not yet love him as he loves you because you have not reached the degree of conformity with his will, you will endure this pain of spending a long while with one who is so different from you when you see how much it benefits you to possess his friendship and how much he loves you (L. 8.5).

I do not know, my Creator, why it is that everyone does not strive to reach you through this special friendship, and why those who are wicked, who are not conformed to your will, do not, in order that you make them good, allow you to be with them at least two hours each day, even though they may not be with you, but with a thousand disturbances from worldly cares and thoughts, as was the case with me (L. 8.6).

As is already known, the examination of conscience, the act of contrition, and the sign of the cross must come first. Then, daughters, since you are alone, strive to find a companion. Well what better companion than the Master himself who taught you this prayer? Represent the Lord himself as close to you and behold how lovingly and humbly he is teaching you. Believe me, you should remain with so good a friend as long as you can. If you grow accustomed to having him present at your side, and he sees that you do so with love and that you go about striving to please him, you will not be able—as they say—to get away from him; he will never fail you; he will help you in all your trials; you will find him everywhere. Do you think it's some small matter to have a friend like this at your side (W. 26.1)?

I'm not asking you now that you think about him or that you draw out a lot of concepts or make long and subtle reflections with your intellect. I'm not asking you to do anything more than look at him. For who can keep you from turning the eyes of your soul toward this Lord, even if you do so just for a moment if you can't do more? You can look at very ugly things; won't you be able to look at the most beautiful thing imaginable? Well now, daughters, your Spouse never takes his eyes off you. He has suffered your committing a thousand ugly offenses and abominations against him, and this suffering wasn't enough for him to cease looking at you. Is it too much to ask you to turn your eyes from these exterior things in order to look at him sometimes? Behold, he is not waiting for anything else, as he says to the bride, than that we look at him. In the measure you desire him, you will find him. He so esteems our turning to look at him that no diligence will be lacking on his part (W. 26.3).

The Prayer of Recollection

This prayer is called "recollection," because the soul collects its faculties together and enters within itself to be with its God. And its divine master comes more quickly to teach it and give it the prayer of quiet than he would through any other method it might use (W. 28.4).

There is a withdrawing of the senses from exterior things and a renunciation of them in such a way that, without one's realizing it, the eyes close so as to avoid seeing them and so that the sight might be more awake to things of the soul.

So, those who walk by this path keep their eyes closed almost as often as they pray. This is a praiseworthy custom for many reasons. It is a striving so as not to look at things here below. This striving comes at the beginning; afterward, there's no need to strive; a greater effort is needed to open the eyes while praying. It seems the soul is aware of being strengthened and fortified at the expense of the body, that it leaves the body alone and weakened, and that it receives in this recollection a supply of provisions to strengthen it against the body.

And even though it isn't aware of this at the beginning, since the recollection is not so deep—for there are greater and lesser degrees of recollection—the soul should get used to this recollection; although in the beginning the body causes difficulty because it claims its rights without realizing that it is cutting off its own head by not surrendering. If we make the effort, practice this recollection for some days, and get used to it, the gain will be clearly seen; we will understand, when beginning to pray, that the bees are approaching and entering the beehive to make honey. And this recollection will be effected without our effort because the Lord has desired that, during the time the faculties are drawn inward, the soul and its will may merit to have this dominion. When the soul does no more than give a sign that it wishes to be recollected, the senses obey it and become recollected. Even though they go out again afterward, their having already surrendered is a great thing; for they go out as captives and subjects and do not cause the harm they did previously. And when the will calls them back again, they come more quickly, until after many of these entries the Lord wills that they rest entirely in perfect contemplation (W. 28.6–8).

The soul can place itself in the presence of Christ and grow accustomed to being inflamed with love for his sacred humanity. It can keep him ever present and speak with him, asking for its needs and complaining of its labors, being glad with him in its enjoyments and not forgetting him because of them, trying to speak to him, not through written prayers but with words that conform to its desires and needs.

This is an excellent way of making progress, and in a very short time. I consider that soul advanced who strives to remain in this precious company and to profit very much by it, and who truly comes to love this Lord to whom we owe so much.

As a result, we shouldn't care at all about not having devotion—as I have said—but we ought to thank the Lord who allows us to be desirous of pleasing him, even though our works may be weak. This method of keeping Christ present with us is beneficial in all stages and is a very safe means of advancing in the first degree of prayer, of reaching in a short time the second degree, and of walking secure against the dangers the devil can set up in the last degrees.

Keeping Christ present is what we of ourselves can do. Whoever would desire to pass beyond this point and raise the spirit to an experience of spiritual delights that are not given would lose both the one and the other, in my opinion; for these consolations belong to the supernatural. And if the intellect is not active, the soul is left very dry, like a desert (L. 12.2–4).

I only wish to inform you that in order to profit by this path and ascend to the dwelling places we desire, the important thing is not to think much but to love much; and so do that which best stirs you to love. Perhaps we don't know what love is. I wouldn't be very surprised, because it doesn't consist in great delight but in desiring with strong determination to please God in everything, in striving, insofar as possible, not to offend him, and in asking him for the advancement of the honor and glory of his Son and the increase of the Catholic Church. These are the signs of love. Don't think the matter lies in thinking of nothing else, and that if you become a little distracted all is lost (IC. IV.1.7).

Chapter 4

The Initial Stages of Contemplation

Passive Recollection

This prayer is something supernatural, something we cannot procure through our own efforts. In it the soul enters into peace or, better, the Lord puts it at peace by his presence . . . (W. 31.2).

The first prayer I experienced that in my opinion was supernatural (a term I use for what cannot be acquired by effort or diligence, however much one tries, although one can dispose oneself for it which would help a great deal) is an interior recollection felt in the soul. For it appears that just as the soul has exterior senses it also has other interior senses through which it seems to want to withdraw within, away from the outside noise. So, sometimes this recollection draws these exterior senses after itself, for it gives the soul the desire to close its eyes and not hear or see or understand anything other than that in which it is then occupied, which is communion with God in solitude. In this state none of the senses or faculties are lost, for all are left intact. But they are left that way so that the soul may be occupied in God. And this explanation will be easy to understand for anyone to whom the Lord has granted this prayer; and for those to whom he has not, there will be need at least for many words and comparisons (ST. 59.3).

But first, I want to mention another kind of prayer . . . It is a recollection that also seems to me to be supernatural because it doesn't involve being in the dark or closing the eyes, nor does it consist in any exterior thing, since without first wanting to do so, one does close one's eyes and desire solitude. . . .

Once the great king, who is in the center dwelling place of this castle, sees their good will, he desires in his wonderful mercy to bring them back to him. Like a good shepherd, with a whistle so gentle that even they themselves almost fail to hear it. He makes them recognize his voice and stops them from going so far astray so that they will return to their dwelling place. And this shepherd's whistle has such power that they abandon the exterior things in which they were estranged from him and enter the castle.

I don't think I've ever explained it as clearly as I have now. When God grants the favor it is a great help to seek him within where he is found more easily and in a way more beneficial to us than when sought in creatures, as Saint Augustine says after having looked for him in many places. Don't think this recollection is acquired by the intellect striving to think about God within itself, or by the imagination imagining him within itself. Such efforts are good and an excellent kind of meditation because they are founded on a truth, which is that God is within us. But this isn't the prayer of recollection because it is something each one can do—with the help of God, as should be understood of everything. But what I'm speaking of comes in a different way. Sometimes before one begins to think of God, these people are already inside the castle. I don't know in what way or how they heard their shepherd's whistle. It wasn't through the ears, because nothing is heard. But one noticeably senses a gentle drawing inward, as anyone who goes through this will observe, for I don't know how to make it clearer. It seems to me I have read where it was compared to a hedgehog curling up or a turtle drawing into a shell. (The one who wrote this example must have understood the experience well.) But these creatures draw inward whenever they want. In the case of this recollection, it doesn't come when we want it but when God wants to grant us the favor. I for myself hold that when His Majesty grants it, he does so to persons who are already beginning to despise the things of the world. I don't say that those in the married state do so in deed, for they cannot, but in desire; for he calls such persons especially so that they might be attentive to interior matters. So I believe that if we desire to make room for His Majesty, he will give not only this but more, and give it to those whom he begins to call to advance further (IC. IV. 3.1–3).

The Prayer of Quiet

The experiences that I call spiritual delight in God, which I termed elsewhere the prayer of quiet, are of a very different kind, as those of you who by the mercy of God have experience of them will know. Let's consider, for a better understanding, that we see two founts with two water troughs. (For I don't find anything more appropriate to explain some spiritual experiences than water; and this is because I know little and have no helpful cleverness of mind and am so fond of this element that I have observed it more attentively than other things. In all the things that so great and wise a God has created there must be many beneficial secrets, and those who understand them do benefit, although I believe that in each little thing created by God there is more than what is understood, even if it is a little ant.)

These two troughs are filled with water in different ways; with one the water comes from far away through many aqueducts and the use of much ingenuity; with the other the source of the water is right there, and the trough fills without any noise. If the spring is abundant, as is this one we are speaking about, the water overflows once the trough is filled, forming a large stream. There is no need of any skill, nor does the building of aqueducts have to continue; but water is always flowing from the spring.

The water coming from the aqueducts is comparable, in my opinion, to the consolations I mentioned that are drawn from meditation. For we obtain them through thoughts, assisting ourselves, using creatures to help our meditation, and tiring the intellect. Since, in the end, the consolation comes through our own efforts, noise is made when there has to be some replenishing of the benefits the consolation causes in the soul, as has been said.

With this other fount, the water comes from its own source which is God. And since His Majesty desires to do so—when he is pleased to grant some supernatural favor—he produces this delight with the greatest peace and quiet and sweetness in the very interior part of ourselves. I don't know from where or how, nor is that happiness and delight experienced, as are earthly consolations, in the heart. I mean there is no similarity at the beginning, for afterward the delight fills everything; this water overflows through all the dwelling places and faculties until reaching the body. This is why I said that it begins in God and ends in ourselves. For, certainly, as anyone who may have experienced it will see, the whole exterior man enjoys this spiritual delight and sweetness.

I was now thinking, while writing this, that the verse mentioned above, *Dilatasti cor meum* [You have enlarged my heart, Ps. 119:32], says the heart was expanded. I don't think the experience is something, as I say, that rises from the heart, but from another part still more interior, as from something deep. I think this must be the center of the soul, as I later came to understand and will mention at the end. For certainly I see secrets within ourselves that have often caused me to marvel. And how many more there must be! Oh, my Lord and my God, how great are your grandeurs! We go about here below like foolish little shepherds, for while it seems that we are getting some knowledge of you it must amount to no more than nothing; for even in our own selves there are great secrets that we don't understand. I say "no more than nothing" because I'm comparing it to the many, many secrets that are in you, not because the grandeurs we see in you are not extraordinary; and that includes those we can attain knowledge of through your works.

To return to the verse, what I think is helpful in it for explaining this matter is the idea of expansion. It seems that since that heavenly water begins to rise from this spring I'm mentioning that is deep within us, it swells and expands our whole interior being, producing ineffable blessings; nor does the soul even understand what is given to it there. It perceives a fragrance, let us say for now as though there were in that interior depth a brazier giving off sweet-smelling perfumes. No light is seen, nor is the place seen where the brazier is; but the warmth and the fragrant fumes spread through the entire soul and even often enough, as I have said, the body shares in them. See now that you understand me; no heat is felt, nor is there the scent of any perfume, for the experience is more delicate than an experience for these things; but I use the examples only so as to explain it to you. And let persons who have not experienced these things understand that truthfully they do happen and are felt in this way, and the soul understands them in a manner clearer than is my explanation right now. This spiritual delight is not something that can be imagined, because however diligent our efforts we cannot acquire it. The very experience of it makes us realize that it is not of the same metal as we ourselves but fashioned from the purest gold of the divine wisdom. Here, in my opinion, the faculties are not united but absorbed and looking as though in wonder at what they see (IC. IV.2.2–6).

Let's leave aside the times when our Lord is pleased to grant it because he wants to and for no other reason. He knows why; we don't have to meddle in this. After you have done what should be done by those in the previous dwelling places: humility! humility! By this means the Lord allows himself to be conquered with regard to anything we want from him. The first sign for seeing whether or not you have humility is that you do not think you deserve these favors and spiritual delights from the Lord or that you will receive them in your lifetime.

You will ask me how then one can obtain them without seeking them. I answer that for the following reasons there is no better way than the one I mentioned, of not striving for them. First, because the initial thing necessary for such favors is to love God without self-interest. Second, because there is a slight lack of humility in thinking that for our miserable services something so great can be obtained. Third, because the authentic preparation for these favors on the part of those of us who, after all have offended him is the desire to suffer and imitate the Lord rather than to have spiritual delights. Fourth, because His Majesty is not obliged to give them to us as he is to give us glory if we keep his commandments. (Without these favors we can be saved, and he knows better than we ourselves what is fitting for us and who of us truly loves him. This is certain, I know. And I know persons who walk by the path of love as they ought to walk, that is, only so as to serve their Christ crucified; not only do these persons refuse to seek spiritual delights from him or to desire them but they beseech him not to give them these favors during their lifetime. This is true.) The fifth reason is that we would be laboring in vain; for since this water must not be drawn through aqueducts as was the previous water, we are little helped by tiring ourselves if the spring doesn't want to produce it. I mean that no matter how much we meditate or how much we try to squeeze something out and have tears, this water doesn't come in such a way. It is given only to whom God wills to give it and often when the soul is least thinking of it.

We belong to him, daughters. Let him do whatever he likes with us, bring us wherever he pleases. I really believe that whoever humbles herself and is detached (I mean in fact because the detachment and humility must not be just in our thoughts—for they often deceive us—but complete) will receive the favor of this water from the Lord and many other favors that we don't know how to desire. May he be forever praised and blessed, amen (IC. IV.2.9–10).

Now let's return to the subject. This quietude and recollection is something that is clearly felt through the satisfaction and peace bestowed on the soul, along with great contentment and calm and a very gentle delight in the faculties. It seems to the soul, since it hasn't gone further, that there's nothing left to desire and that it should willingly say with Saint Peter that it will make its dwelling there. It dares not move or stir, for it seems that good will slip through it hands—nor would it even want to breathe sometimes. The poor little thing doesn't understand that since by its own efforts it can do nothing to draw that good to itself, so much less will it be able to keep it for longer than the Lord desires.

I have already mentioned that in this first recollection and quiet the soul's faculties do not cease functioning. But the soul is so satisfied with God that as long as the recollection lasts, the quiet and calm are not lost since the will is united with God even though the two faculties are distracted; in fact, little by little the will brings the intellect and the memory back to recollection. Because even though the will may not be totally absorbed, it is so well occupied, without knowing how, that no matter what efforts the other two faculties make, they cannot take away its contentment and joy. But rather with hardly any effort the will is gradually helped so that this little spark of love of God may not go out.

May it please His Majesty to give me grace to explain this state well because there are many, many souls who reach it but few that pass beyond; and I don't know whose fault it is. Most surely God does not fail, for once His Majesty has granted a soul the favor of reaching this stage, I don't believe he will fail to grant it many more favors unless through its own fault (L. 15.1–2).

This prayer, then, is a little spark of the Lord's true love which he begins to enkindle in the soul; and he desires that the soul grow in the understanding of what this love accompanied by delight is. For anyone who has experience, it is impossible not to understand soon that this little spark cannot be acquired. Yet, this nature of ours is so eager for delights that it tries everything; but it is quickly left cold because however much it may desire to light the fire and obtain this delight, it doesn't seem to be doing anything else than throwing water on it and killing it. If this quietude and recollection and little spark is from God's spirit and not a delight given by the devil or procured by ourselves, it will be noticed no matter how small it is. And if we don't extinguish it through our own fault, it is what will begin to enkindle the large fire that (as I mention in its place) throws forth flames of the greatest love of God which His Majesty gives to perfect souls (L. 15.4).

What the soul must do during these times of quiet amounts to no more than proceeding gently and noiselessly. What I call noise is running about with the intellect looking for many words and reflections so as to give thanks for this gift and piling up one's sins and faults in order to see that the gift is unmerited. Everything is motion here; the intellect is representing, and the memory hurrying about. For certainly these faculties tire me out from time to time; and although I have a poor memory, I cannot subdue it. The will calmly and wisely must understand that one does not deal well with God by force and that our efforts are like the careless use of large pieces of wood which smother this little spark. One should realize this and humbly say; "Lord, what am I capable of here? What has the servant to do with the Lord—or earth with heaven?" Or other words that at this time come to mind out of love and well grounded in the knowledge that what is said is the truth. And one should pay no attention to the intellect, for it is a grinding mill. The will may desire to share what it enjoys or may work to recollect the intellect, for often it will find itself in this union and calm while the intellect wanders about aimlessly. It is better that the will leave the intellect alone than go after it, and that it remain like a wise bee in the recollection and in enjoyment of that gift. For if no bee were to enter the beehive and each were employed in going after the other, no honey could be made

As a result, the soul will lose a great deal if it isn't careful in this matter, especially if the intellect is keen. For when the soul begins to compose speeches and search for ideas, though insignificant, it will think it is doing something if they are well expressed. The idea it should have here is a clear understanding that there isn't any idea that will make God give us so great a favor but that this favor comes only from his goodness; and it should be aware that we are very near His Majesty and ask for his gifts and pray for the Church and for those who have asked for our prayers and for the souls in purgatory, not with the noise of words but with longing that he hear us. This is a kind of prayer that includes many things and in which more is obtained than through a great deal of reflection by the intellect. Let the will awaken within itself some spontaneous considerations verifying its progress so as to quicken this love, and let it make some loving acts about what it will do for one to whom it owes so much without, as I said, admitting noise from the intellect which goes about looking for great concepts. In fact, a little straw put there with humility—and it will be less than a straw if we put it on ourselves—will serve the purpose and help more to enkindle the fire than a lot of wood along with much learned reasoning. These, in our opinion, would smother the spark within the space of a creed.

This advice is good for the learned men who ordered me to write. For, through the goodness of God, all may reach this prayer; and it may happen that these learned men will pass the time in making scriptural applications. Although their studies will not cease to benefit them a lot before and afterward, here during these periods of prayer there is little need for learning, in my opinion; rather, their studies will make the will tepid. For in seeing itself near the light, the intellect then has the greatest clarity; and I, though being what I am, seem to be another person (L. 15.6–7).

From this prayer there usually proceeds what is called a sleep of the faculties, for they are neither absorbed nor so suspended that the prayer can be called a rapture. Although this prayer is not complete union, the soul sometimes, and even often, understands that the will alone is united, and this is known very clearly; I mean it is clear in the soul's opinion. The will is completely occupied in God, and it sees it lacks the power to be engaged in any other work. The other two faculties are free for business and works of service of God. In sum, Martha and Mary walk together. I asked Father Francis [Saint Francis Borgia] if this experience could be deceiving because it puzzled me, and he told me that the experience is a frequent one (ST. 59.5).

Chapter 5

Pure Contemplation

The Prayer of Union

When there is union of all the faculties, things are very different because none of them is able to function. The intellect is as though in awe; the will loves more than it understands, but it doesn't understand in a describable way whether it loves or what it does; there is no memory at all, in my opinion, nor thought; nor even during that time are the senses awake, but they are as though lost, that the soul might be more occupied in what it enjoys. This union passes quickly. By the wealth of humility and other virtues and desires left in the soul, one discerns the great good that comes to one through that favor. But what the union is cannot be described, for even though the soul is given understanding, it doesn't know how it understands or how to describe it. In my opinion, if this experience is authentic, it is the greatest favor our Lord grants along this spiritual path, at least among the greatest (ST. 59.6).

Yet few of us dispose ourselves that the Lord may communicate it to us. In exterior matters we are proceeding well so that we will reach what is necessary; but in the practice of the virtues that are necessary for arriving at this point we need very, very much and cannot be careless in either small things or great. So, my sisters, since in some way we can enjoy heaven on earth, be brave in begging the Lord to give us his grace in such a way that nothing will be lacking through our own fault; that God show us the way and strengthen the soul that it may dig until it finds this hidden treasure. The truth is that the treasure lies within our very selves. This is what I would like to know how to explain, if the Lord would enable me to do so.

I said "strengthen the soul" so that you will understand that bodily strength is not necessary for those to whom God does not give it. God doesn't make it impossible for anyone to buy his riches. He is content if each one gives what he has. Blessed be so great a God. But reflect, daughters, that he doesn't want you to hold on to anything, so that you will be able to enjoy the favors we are speaking of. Whether you have little or much, God wants everything for himself; and in conformity with what you know you have given you will receive greater or lesser favors. There is no better proof for recognizing whether our prayer has reached union or not (IC. V.1.2–3).

There is no need here to use any technique to suspend the mind since all the faculties are asleep in this state—and truly asleep—to the things of the world and to ourselves. As a matter of fact, during the time that the union lasts the soul is left as though without its senses, for it has no power to think even if it wants to. In loving, if it does love, it doesn't understand how or what it is it loves or what it would want. In sum, it is like one who in every respect has died to the world so as to live more completely in God (IC. V.1.4).

It seems to me that you're still not satisfied, for you will think you can be mistaken and that these interior things are something difficult to examine. What was said will be sufficient for anyone who has experienced union. Yet, because the difference between union and the previous experience is great, I want to mention a clear sign by which you will be sure against error or doubts about whether the union is from God. His Majesty has brought it to my memory today, and in my opinion it is the sure sign. . . .

Well then, to return to the sign that I say is the true one, you now see that God has made this soul a fool with regard to all so as better to impress upon it true wisdom. For during the time of this union it neither sees, nor hears, nor understands, because the union is always short and seems to the soul even much shorter than it probably is. God so places himself in the interior of that soul that when it returns to itself it can in no way doubt that it was in God and God was in it. This truth remains with it so firmly that even though years go by without God's granting that favor again, the soul can neither forget nor doubt that it was in God and God was in it (IC. V.1.7.9).

And I would say that whoever does not receive this certitude does not experience union of the whole soul with God, but union of some faculty, or that he experiences one of the many other kinds of favors God grants souls. In regard to all these favors we have to give up looking for reasons to see how they've come about. Since our intellect cannot understand this union why do we have to make this effort? It's enough for us to see that he who is the cause of it is almighty. Since we have no part at all to play in bringing it about no matter how much effort we put forth, but it is God who does so, let us not desire the capacity to understand this union.

Now I recall, in saying that we have no part to play, what you have heard the bride say in the Song of Songs: he brought me into the wine cellar (or, placed me there, I believe it says) [Sg. 2:4]. And it doesn't say that she went. And it says also that she went looking about in every part of the city for her beloved [Sg. 3:2]. I understand this union to be the wine cellar where the Lord wishes to place us when he desires and as he desires. But however great the effort we make to do so, we cannot enter. His Majesty must place us there and enter himself into the center of our soul. And that he may show his marvels more clearly he doesn't want our will to have any part to play, for it has been entirely surrendered to him. Neither does he want the door of the faculties and of the senses to be opened, for they are all asleep. But he wants to enter the center of the soul without going through any door, as he entered the place where his disciples were when he said, *pax vobis;* or as he left the tomb without lifting away the stone. Further on you will see in the last dwelling place how His Majesty desires that the soul enjoy him in its own center even much more than here (IC. V.1.11–12).

It seems to me that despite all I've said about this dwelling place, the matter is still somewhat obscure. Since so much gain comes from entering this place, it will be good to avoid giving the impression that those to whom the Lord doesn't give things that are so supernatural are left without hope. True union can very well be reached, with God's help, if we make the effort to obtain it by keeping our wills fixed only on that which is God's will (IC. V.3.3).

What do you think his will is, daughters? That we be completely perfect. See what we lack to be one with him and his Father as His Majesty asked. I tell you I am writing this with much pain upon seeing myself so far away—and all through my own fault. The Lord doesn't have to grant us great delights for this union; sufficient is what he has given us in his Son, who would teach us the way. Don't think the matter lies in my being so conformed to the will of God that if my father or brother dies I don't feel it, or that if there are trials or sicknesses I suffer them happily. Such an attitude is good, and sometimes it's a matter of discretion because we can't do otherwise, and we make a virtue of necessity. How many things like these the philosophers did, or even, though not like these, other things, such as acquiring much learning. Here in our religious life the Lord asks of us only two things: love of His Majesty and love of our neighbor. These are what we must work for. By observing them with perfection, we do his will and so will be united with him. But how far, as I have said, we are from doing these two things for so great a God as we ought! May it please His Majesty to give us his grace so that we might merit, if we want, to reach this state that lies within our power (IC. V.3.7).

Oh, sisters, how clearly one sees the degree to which love of neighbor is present in some of you, and how clearly one sees the deficiency in those who lack such perfection! If you were to understand how important this virtue is for us you wouldn't engage in any other study.

When I see souls very earnest in trying to understand the prayer they have and very sullen when they are in it—for it seems they don't dare let their minds move or stir lest a bit of their spiritual delight and devotion be lost—it makes me realize how little they understand of the way by which union is attained; they think the whole matter lies in these things. No, sisters, absolutely not; works are what the Lord wants! He desires that if you see a sister who is sick to whom you can bring some relief, you have compassion on her and not worry about losing this devotion; and that if she is suffering pain, you also feel it; and that, if necessary, you fast so that she might eat—not so much for her sake as because you know it is your Lord's desire. This is true union with his will, and if you see a person praised, the Lord wants you to be much happier than if you yourself were being praised. This, indeed, is easy, for if you have humility you will feel sorry to see yourself praised. But this happiness that comes when the virtues of the sisters are known is a very good thing; and when we see some fault in them, it is also a very good thing to be sorry and hide the fault as though it were our own.

I have said a lot on this subject elsewhere, because I see, sisters, that if we fail in love of neighbor we are lost. May it please the Lord that this will never be so; for if you do not fail, I tell you that you shall receive from His Majesty the union that was mentioned. When you see yourselves lacking in this love, even though you have devotion and gratifying experiences that make you think you have reached this stage, and you experience some little suspension in the prayer of quiet (for to some it then appears that everything has been accomplished), believe me you have not reached union. And beg our Lord to give you this perfect love of neighbor. Let His Majesty have a free hand, for he will give you more than you know how to desire because you are striving and making every effort to do what you can about this love. And force your will to do the will of your sisters in everything even though you may lose your rights; forget your own good for their sakes no matter how much resistance your nature puts up; and, when the occasion arises, strive to accept work yourself so as to relieve your neighbor of it. Don't think that it won't cost you anything or that you will find everything done for you. Look at what our Spouse's love for us cost him; in order to free us from death, he died that most painful death of the cross (IC. V.3.10–12).

Spiritual Betrothal

It seems to me that the prayer of union does not yet reach the stage of spiritual betrothal. Here below when two people are to be engaged, there is a discussion about whether they are alike, whether they love each other, and whether they might meet together so as to become more satisfied with each other. So, too, in the case of this union with God, the agreement has been made, and this soul is well informed about the goodness of her Spouse and determined to do his will in everything and in as many ways as she sees might make him happy. And His Majesty, as one who understands clearly whether these things about his betrothed are so, is happy with her. As a result he grants this mercy, for he desired her to know him more and that they might meet together, as they say, and be united. We can say that union is like this, for it passes in a very short time (IC IV.4.4).

That meeting left such an impression that the soul's whole desire is to enjoy it again. I have already said that in this prayer nothing is seen in a way that can be called seeing, nor is anything seen with the imagination. I use the term "meeting" because of the comparison I made. Now the soul is fully determined to take no other spouse. But the Spouse does not look at the soul's great desires that the betrothal take place, for he still wants it to desire this more, and he wants the betrothal to take place at a cost; it is the greatest of blessings. And although everything is small when it comes to paying for this exceptional benefit, I tell you, daughters, that for the soul to endure such delay it needs to have that token or pledge of betrothal that it now has (IC. VI.1.1).

Well let us begin, then, to discuss the manner in which the Spouse deals with it and how before he belongs to it completely he makes it desire him vehemently by certain delicate means the soul itself does not understand. (Nor do I believe I'll be successful in explaining them save to those who have experienced them.) These are impulses so delicate and refined, for they proceed from very deep within the interior part of the soul, that I don't know any comparison that will fit (IC. VI.2.1).

God has another way of awakening the soul. Although it somehow seems to be a greater favor than those mentioned, it can be more dangerous, and therefore I shall pause a little to consider it. There are many kinds of locutions given to the soul. Some seem to come from outside oneself; others, from deep within the interior part of the soul; others, from the superior part; and some are so exterior that they come through the sense of hearing, for it seems there is a spoken word. Sometimes, and often, the locution can be an illusion, especially in persons with a weak imagination or in those who are melancholic, I mean who suffer noticeably from melancholy (IC. VI.3.1).

One thing very certain is that when the spirit is from God the soul esteems itself less, the greater the favor granted, and it has more awareness of its sins and is more forgetful of its own gain, and its will and memory are employed more in seeking only the honor of God, nor does it think about its own profit, and it walks with greater fear lest its will deviate in anything, and with greater certitude that it never deserved any of those favors but deserved hell. Since all the favors and things it experienced in prayer produce these effects, the soul does not walk fearfully but with confidence in the mercy of the Lord, who is faithful and will not let the devil deceive it; although walking with fear is always good (IC. VI.3.17).

I should like to know how to explain, with God's help, the difference there is between union and rapture, or, as they call it, elevation or flight of the spirit, or transport, which are all the same. I mean that these latter terms, though different, refer to the same thing; it is also called ecstasy. The advantage rapture has over union is great. The rapture produces much stronger effects and causes many other phenomena. Union seems the same at the beginning, in the middle, and at the end; and it takes place in the interior of the soul. But since these other phenomena are of a higher degree, they produce their effect both interiorly and exteriorly. May the Lord explain as he did for the other degrees. Certainly, if His Majesty had not given me an understanding of the manners and ways in which something could be said about them, I would not have known how to speak of them (L. 20.1).

The union, as I understand it, is different from the elevation. It will seem to anyone who may not have experienced this elevation of the spirit that there is no difference between the two; but, in my opinion, though they are one, the Lord works differently in each case. And in the flight of the spirit this difference is seen by a much greater increase in detachment from creatures. I have perceived clearly that the elevation of the spirit is a particular favor, even though as I say it may be the same as union or appear to be so. A small fire is just as much a fire as is a large one. Through this example one can see the difference there is between union and elevation of the spirit. In a small fire it takes a lot of time for a piece of iron to become red-hot. But if the fire is great, the piece of iron, even though large, will in a short time lose its entire being—or it will appear to do so. This example, it seems to me, shows what the difference between the two favors from the Lord is like. I know that anyone who has reached the experience of raptures will understand the difference well. To one who has no experience the explanation will seem confusing, and it could well be. It is not surprising that there is confusion when a person like myself wants to speak of such a thing and to give some explanation of an experience that it seems one cannot even begin to put into words (L. 18.7).

Rapture and suspension, in my opinion, are both the same. But I am used to saying suspension in order to avoid saying rapture, a word that frightens. And indeed the union just described can also be called suspension. The difference between rapture and union is this: the rapture lasts longer and is felt more exteriorly, for your breathing diminishes in such a way that you are unable to speak or open your eyes. Although this diminishing of these bodily powers occurs in union, it takes place in this prayer with greater force, because the natural heat leaves the body, going I don't know where. When the rapture is intense (for in all these kinds of prayer there is a more and a less), when it is greater, as I say, the hands are frozen and sometimes stretched out like sticks, and the body remains as it is, either standing or kneeling. And the soul is so occupied with rejoicing in what the Lord represents to it that it seemingly forgets to animate the body and leaves the body abandoned; and if the suspension lasts, the nerves are left aching.

It seems to me the Lord here wants the soul to understand more of what it enjoys in the union. So some things about His Majesty are usually revealed to it in the rapture. And the effects left in the soul are great, and there is a forgetfulness of self in the desire that so tremendous a Lord and God be known and praised. In my opinion, if the suspension is from God the soul cannot remain without a deep awareness of its inability to do anything there and of its great misery and ingratitude for not having served him who solely out of his goodness grants it such a wonderful favor. For the feeling and sweetness are so excessive that if the remembrance of them didn't pass away, all the comparable satisfactions here on earth would ever be nauseating to the soul. As a result, it comes to have little esteem for all the things of the world (ST. 59.7–8).

When the soul is in this suspension, the Lord likes to show it some secrets, things about heaven, and imaginative visions. It is able to tell of them afterward, for these remain so impressed on the memory that they are never forgotten. But when the visions are intellectual, the soul doesn't know how to speak of them. For there must be some visions during these moments that are so sublime that it's not fitting for those who live on this earth to have the further understanding necessary to explain them. However, when the soul is again in possession of its senses, it can say many things about these intellectual visions. It could be that some of you do not know what a vision is, especially an intellectual one. I shall explain at the proper time, for one who has the authority ordered me to do so. And although the explanation may not seem pertinent, it will perhaps benefit some souls.

Well now you will ask me: if afterward there is to be no remembrance of these sublime favors granted by the Lord to the soul in this state, what benefit do they have? Oh, daughters, they are so great one cannot exaggerate! For even though they are unexplainable, they are well inscribed in the very interior part of the soul and are never forgotten.

But, you will insist, if there is no image and the faculties do not understand, how can the visions be remembered? I don't understand this either; but I do understand that some truths about the grandeur of God remain so fixed in this soul, that even if faith were not to tell it who God is and of its obligation to believe that he is God, from that very moment it would adore him as God, as did Jacob when he saw the ladder. By means of the ladder Jacob must have understood other secrets that he didn't know how to explain, for by seeing just a ladder on which angels descended and ascended he would not have understood such great mysteries if there had not been deeper interior enlightenment [Gn. 28:12]. I don't know if I'm guessing right in what I say, for although I have heard this story about Jacob, I don't know if I'm remembering it correctly.

Nor did Moses know how to describe all that he saw in the bush, but only what God wished him to describe [Ex. 3:1–16]. But if God had not shown secrets to his soul along with a certitude that made him recognize and believe that they were from God, Moses could not have entered into so many severe trials. But he must have understood such deep things among the thorns of that bush that the vision gave him the courage to do what he did for the people of Israel. So, sisters, we don't have to look for reasons to understand the hidden things of God. Since we believe he is powerful, clearly we must believe that a worm with as limited a power as ours will not understand his grandeurs. Let us praise him, for he is pleased that we come to know some of them.

I have been wanting to find some comparison by which to explain what I'm speaking about, and I don't think there is any that fits. But let's use this one: you enter into the room of a king or great lord, or I believe they call it the treasure chamber, where there are countless kinds of glass and earthen vessels and other things so arranged that almost all these objects are seen upon entering. Once I was brought to a room like this in the house of the Duchess of Alba where, while I was on a journey, obedience ordered me to stay because of this lady's insistence with my superiors. I was amazed on entering and wondered what benefit could be gained from the conglomeration of things, and I saw that one could praise the Lord at seeing so many different kinds of objects, and now I laugh to myself upon realizing how the experience has helped me here in my explanation. Although I was in that room for a while, there was so much there to see that I soon forgot it all; none of those pieces has remained in my memory any more than if I had never seen them, nor would I know how to explain the workmanship of any of them. I can only say in general that I remember seeing everything. Likewise with this favor, the soul, while it is made one with God, is placed in this room of the empyreal heaven that we must have interiorly. For clearly, the soul has some of these dwelling places since God abides within it. And although the Lord must not want the soul to see these secrets every time it is in this ecstasy, for it can be so absorbed in enjoying him that a sublime good like that is sufficient for it, sometimes he is pleased that the absorption decrease and the soul see at once what is in that room. After it returns to itself, the soul is left with that representation of the grandeurs it saw; but it cannot describe any of them, nor do its natural powers attain to any more than what God wished that it see supernaturally.

You, therefore, might object that I admit that the soul sees and that the vision is an imaginative one. But I'm not saying that, for

I'm not dealing with an imaginative vision but with an intellectual one. Since I have no learning, I don't know how in my dullness to explain anything. If what I have said up to now about this prayer is worthwhile, I know clearly that I'm not the one who has said it.

I hold that if at times in its raptures the soul doesn't understand these secrets, its raptures are not given by God but caused by some natural weakness. It can happen to persons with a weak constitution that any spiritual force will overcome the natural powers, and the soul will be absorbed as I believe I mentioned in reference to the prayer of quiet. These experiences have nothing to do with rapture. In a rapture, believe me, God carries off for himself the entire soul, and, as to someone who is his own and his spouse, he begins showing it some little part of the kingdom that it has gained by being espoused to him. However small that part of his kingdom may be, everything that there is in this great God is magnificent. And he doesn't want any hindrance from anyone, neither from the faculties nor from the senses, but he immediately commands the doors of all these dwelling places to be closed; and only that door to his dwelling place remains open so that we can enter. Blessed be so much mercy; they will be rightly cursed who have not wanted to benefit by it and who have lost this Lord (IC. VI.4.5–10).

Three things, especially, are left in it to a very sublime degree: knowledge of the grandeur of God, because the more we see in this grandeur the greater is our understanding; self-knowledge and humility upon seeing that something so low in comparison with the Creator of so many grandeurs dared to offend him (and neither does the soul dare look up at him); the third, little esteem of earthly things save for those that can be used for the service of so great a God.

These are the jewels the Spouse begins to give the betrothed, and their value is such that the soul will not want to lose them (IC. VI.5.10–11).

I know a person or two persons—one was a man—to whom the Lord had granted some of these favors, who were so desirous of serving His Majesty at their own cost, without these great delights, and so anxious to suffer that they complained to our Lord because he bestowed the favors on them, and if they could decline receiving these gifts they would do so. I am speaking not of the delights coming from these visions—for in the end these persons see that the visions are very beneficial and to be highly esteemed—but of those the Lord gives in contemplation (IC. VI.9.17).

It is true that these desires also, in my opinion, are supernatural and characteristic of souls very much inflamed in love. Such souls would want the Lord to see that they do not serve him for pay. Thus, as I have said, they never, as a motive for making the effort to serve more, think about receiving glory for anything they do. But their desire is to satisfy love, and it is love's nature to serve with deeds in a thousand ways. If it could, love would want to discover ways of consuming the soul within itself. And if it were necessary to be always annihilated for the greater honor of God, love would do so very eagerly. May he be praised forever, amen. For in lowering himself to commune with such miserable creatures, he wants to show his greatness (IC VI.9.18).

The Spiritual Marriage

Now then, when His Majesty is pleased to grant the soul this divine marriage that was mentioned, he first brings it into his own dwelling place. . . .

In this seventh dwelling place the union comes about in a different way: our good God now desires to remove the scales from the soul's eyes and let it see and understand, although in a strange way, something of the favor he grants it. When the soul is brought into that dwelling place, the Most Blessed Trinity, all three Persons, through an intellectual vision, is revealed to it through a certain representation of the truth. First there comes an enkindling in the spirit in the manner of a cloud of magnificent splendor; and these Persons are distinct, and through an admirable knowledge the soul understands as a most profound truth that all three Persons are one substance and one power and one knowledge and one God alone. It knows in such a way that what we hold by faith, it understands, we can say, through sight—although the sight is not with the bodily eyes or with the eyes of the soul, because we are not dealing with an imaginative vision. Here all three Persons communicate themselves to it, speak to it, and explain those words of the Lord in the gospel: that he and the Father and the Holy Spirit will come to dwell with the soul that loves him and keeps his commandments.

Oh, God help me! How different is hearing and believing these words from understanding their truth in this way! Each day this soul becomes more amazed, for these Persons never seem to leave it any more, but it clearly beholds, in the way that was mentioned, that they are within it. In the extreme interior, in some place very deep within itself, the nature of which it doesn't know how to explain, because of a lack of learning, it perceives this divine company.

You may think that as a result the soul will be outside itself and so absorbed that it will be unable to be occupied with anything else. On the contrary, the soul is much more occupied than before with everything pertaining to the service of God; and once its duties are over it remains with that enjoyable company. If the soul does not fail God, he will never fail, in my opinion, to make his presence clearly known to it. It has strong confidence that since God has granted this favor he will not allow it to lose the favor. Though the soul thinks this, it goes about with greater care than ever not to displease him in anything.

It should be understood that this presence is not felt so fully, I mean so clearly, as when revealed the first time or at other times when God grants the soul this gift. For if the presence were felt so clearly, the soul would find it impossible to be engaged in anything else or even to live among people. But even though the presence is not perceived with this very clear light, the soul finds itself in this company every time it takes notice. Let's say that the experience resembles that of a person who after being in a bright room with others finds herself, once the shutters are closed, in darkness. The light by which she could see them is taken away. Until it returns she doesn't see them, but not for that reason does she stop knowing they are present. It might be asked whether the soul can see them when it so desires and the light returns. To see them does not lie in its power, but depends on when our Lord desires that the window of the intellect be opened. Great is the mercy he shows in never departing from the soul and in desiring that it perceive him so manifestly (IC. VII.1.5–10).

And that its life is Christ [Phil. 1:2] is understood better, with the passing of time, by the effects this life has. Through some secret aspirations the soul understands clearly that it is God who gives life to our soul. These aspirations come very, very often in such a living way that they can in no way be doubted. The soul feels them very clearly even though they are indescribable. But the feeling is so powerful that sometimes the soul cannot avoid the loving expressions they cause, such as: O Life of my life! Sustenance that sustains me! and things of this sort. . . . For just as a great gush of water could not reach us if it didn't have a source, as I have said, so it is understood clearly that there is Someone in the interior depths who shoots these arrows and gives life to this life, and that there is a Sun in the interior of the soul from which a brilliant light proceeds and is sent to the faculties. The soul, as I have said, does not move from that center nor is its peace lost; for the very One who gave peace to the apostles when they were together [Jn. 20:19–21] can give it to the soul (IC. VII.2.6).

We have always seen that those who were closer to Christ our Lord were those with the greatest trials. Let us look at what his glorious mother suffered and the glorious apostles. How do you think Saint Paul could have suffered such very great trials? Through him we can see the effects visions and contemplation produce when from our Lord, and not from the imagination or the devil's deceit. Did Saint Paul by chance hide himself in the enjoyment of these delights and not engage in anything else? You already see that he didn't have a day of rest, from what we can understand, and neither did he have any rest at night since it was then that he earned his livelihood. I like very much the account about Saint Peter fleeing from prison and how our Lord appeared to him and told him, "I am on my way to Rome to be crucified again." We never recite the office of this feast, where this account is, that I don't find particular consolation. How did this favor from the Lord impress Saint Peter or what did he do? He went straight to his death. And it was no small mercy from the Lord that Peter found someone to provide him with death.

O my sisters! How forgetful this soul, in which the Lord dwells in so particular a way, should be of its own rest, how little it should care for its honor, and how far it should be from wanting esteem in anything! For if it is with him very much, as is right, it should think little about itself. All its concern is taken up with how to please him more and how or where it will show him the love it bears him. This is the reason for prayer, my daughters, the purpose of this spiritual marriage: the birth always of good works, good works [IC. VII.4.5–6].

Part 2

Glimmerings from the Divine Depths

Chapter 6

The Inner World of Beauty and Ugliness

Among the objects of her contemplation Teresa's own soul stands in a prominent place. Previous to her contemplative experiences, her knowledge of the human soul was vague and general. She knew little of what the contemporary philosophy or theology had to say about its powers, depth, and structure, or about its relations with the divinity, with God present and immanent. She had never imagined the human being's rich potentiality for deification, for sharing through the divine bounty in all that God possesses. Life and soul, often limited to an earthly horizon, are revealed to her as open to the beauty and wonders of God, to a heavenly, eternal life. Ultimately, by soul Teresa means the person. Subjectively, the soul corresponds to our I, but with a nuance of interiority and living power. Yet persons are free and can refuse the offer of God's self-communication, they can choose ugliness over beauty.

Today while beseeching our Lord to speak for me because I wasn't able to think of anything to say nor did I know how to begin to carry out this obedience, there came to my mind what I shall now speak about, that which will provide us with a basis to begin with. It is that we consider our soul to be like a castle made entirely out of a diamond or of very clear crystal, in which there are many rooms, just as in heaven there are many dwelling places. For in reflecting upon it carefully, sisters, we realize that the soul of the just person is nothing else but a paradise where the Lord says he finds his delight. So then, what do you think that abode will be like where a king so powerful, so wise, so pure, so full of all good things takes his delight? I don't find anything comparable to the magnificent beauty of a soul and its marvelous capacity. Indeed, our intellects, however keen, can hardly comprehend it, just as they cannot comprehend God; but he himself says that he created us in his own image and likeness (IC I.1.1).

I know a person to whom our Lord wanted to show what a soul in mortal sin was like. That person says that in her opinion if this were understood it would be impossible to sin, even though a soul would have to undergo the greatest trials imaginable in order to flee the occasions. So the Lord gave her a strong desire that all might understand this. May he give you, daughters, the desire to beseech him earnestly for those who are in this state, who have become total darkness, and whose works have become darkness also. For just as all the streams that flow from a crystal-clear fount are also clear, the works of a soul in grace, because they proceed from this fount of life, in which the soul is planted like a tree, are most pleasing in the eyes of both God and man. There would be no freshness, no fruit, if it were not for this fount sustaining the tree, preventing it from drying up, and causing it to produce good fruit. Thus in the case of a soul that through its own fault withdraws from this fount and plants itself in a place where the water is black and foul-smelling, everything that flows from it is equally wretched and filthy.

It should be kept in mind here that the fount, the shining sun that is in the center of the soul, does not lose its beauty and splendor; it is always present in the soul, and nothing can take away its loveliness. But if a black cloth is placed over a crystal that is in the sun, obviously the sun's brilliance will have no effect on the crystal even though the sun is shining on it.

O souls redeemed by the blood of Jesus Christ! Understand and take pity on yourselves. How is it possible that in realizing these things you don't strive to remove the pitch from this crystal? (IC. I. 2.2–4).

Well, let us imagine that within us is an extremely rich palace, built entirely of gold and precious stones; in sum, built for a lord such as this. Imagine, too, as is indeed so, that you have a part to play in order for the palace to be so beautiful; for there is no edifice as beautiful as is a soul pure and full of virtues. The greater the virtues the more resplendent the jewels. Imagine, also, that in this palace dwells this mighty king who has been gracious enough to become your father; and that he is seated upon an extremely valuable throne, which is your heart.

This may seem trifling at the beginning; I mean, this image I've used in order to explain recollection. But the image may be very helpful—to you especially—for since we women have no learning, all of this imagining is necessary that we may truly understand that within us lies something incomparably more precious than what we see outside ourselves. Let's not imagine that we are hollow inside. And please God it may be only women that go about forgetful of this inner richness and beauty. I consider it impossible for us to pay so much attention to worldly things if we take the care to remember we have a guest such as this within us, for we then see how lowly these things are next to what we possess within ourselves. Well, what else does an animal do upon seeing what is pleasing to its sight than satisfy its hunger by taking the prey? Indeed, there should be some difference between them and us.

You will laugh at me, perhaps, and say that what I'm explaining is very clear, and you'll be right; for me, though, it was obscure for some time. I understood well that I had a soul. But what this soul deserved and who dwelt within it, I did not understand because I had covered my eyes with the vanities of the world. For, in my opinion, if I had understood as I do now that in this little palace of my soul dwelt so great a king, I would not have left him alone so often. I would have remained with him at times and striven more so as not to be so unclean. But what a marvelous thing, that he who would fill a thousand worlds and many more with his grandeur would enclose himself in something so small! In fact, since he is Lord he is free to do what he wants, and since he loves us he adapts himself to our size (W. 28.9–11).

Once while I was reciting with all the sisters the hours of the Divine Office, my soul suddenly became recollected; and it seemed to me to be like a brightly polished mirror, without any part on the back or sides or top or bottom that wasn't totally clear. In its center Christ, our Lord, was shown to me, in the way I usually see him. It seemed to me I saw him clearly in every part of my soul, as though in a mirror. And this mirror also—I don't know how to explain it—was completely engraved upon the Lord himself by means of a very loving communication I wouldn't know how to describe. I know that this vision is very beneficial to me each time I remember it, especially after receiving Communion. I was given understanding of what it is for a soul to be in mortal sin. It amounts to clouding this mirror with mist and leaving it black; and thus this Lord cannot be revealed or seen, even though he is always present giving us being. And I understood that heresies amount to breaking the mirror; which is much worse than its being darkened. The way in which this is seen is very different from telling about it because it can be poorly described. But it brought me much profit and caused me grief for the times in which through my sins I so darkened my soul that I couldn't see this Lord.

I think this vision is advantageous to recollected persons, in teaching them to consider the Lord as very deep within their souls; such a thought is much more alluring and fruitful than thinking of him as outside oneself, as I mentioned at other times. And some books on prayer tell about where one must seek God. Particularly, the glorious Saint Augustine speaks about this for neither in the market place nor in pleasures nor anywhere else that he sought God did he find him as he did when he sought him within himself. Within oneself, very clearly, is the best place to look; and it's not necessary to go to heaven, nor any further than our own selves; for to do so is to tire the spirit and distract the soul, without gaining as much fruit (L. 40.5–6).

Once while I was recollected in this company I always bear with me in my soul, God seemed so present to me that I thought of Saint Peter's words: "You are Christ, Son of the living God" [Mt. 16:16]. For God was thus living in my soul. This presence is not like other visions, because it is accompanied by such living faith that one cannot doubt that the Trinity is in our souls by presence, power, and essence. It is an extremely beneficial thing to understand this truth. Since I was amazed to see such majesty in something so lowly as my soul, I heard: "It is not lowly, daughter, for it is made in my image." I also understood some things about why God delights to be with souls more than with other creatures. These matters were so subtle that even though my intellect understood them immediately, I shall not be able to explain them (ST. 49).

Chapter 7

God Omnipresent and True

God's Omnipresence

God is not only the most high; he is the all-near God as well. He is the supreme being but never isolated from the world by his perfection. Teresa's discovery—a remarkable and wonderful surprise for her—of the presence of God within every soul, of the divine immanence as well as transcendence, also came in the light of a series of contemplative graces. Furthermore, she learned that God is supremely immanent only because he is supremely transcendent, not limited by anything finite, and thus that God is in all things as containing them, that all things are in God. The presence of God is not material however. If this presence manifests itself through sensible signs, it is still the presence of a spiritual being whose love envelops his creature and vivifies it, whose love wishes to communicate itself to the people of the earth and make of them a luminous witness of his presence.

In the beginning I was ignorant about a certain matter because I didn't know that God was in all things, and though he seemed to be present to me, I thought this omnipresence was impossible. I couldn't stop believing that he was there since it seemed to me that I understood almost clearly that he was there by his very presence. Those who had no learning told me that he was present only by grace. I couldn't believe this, because, as I say, it seemed to me he was present; and so I was troubled. A very learned man from the order of the glorious Saint Dominic freed me from this doubt, for he told me that God was present and of how God communicates himself to us; these truths consoled me tremendously (L. 18.15).

Now, you will ask me, how did the soul see this truth or understand if it didn't see or understand anything? I don't say that it then saw the truth but that afterward it sees the truth clearly, not because of a vision but because of a certitude remaining in the soul that only God can place there. I know a person who hadn't learned that God was in all things by presence, power, and essence, and through a favor of this kind that God granted her she came to believe it. After asking a half-learned man of the kind I mentioned—he knew as little as she had known before God enlightened her—she was told that God was present only by grace. Such was her own conviction that even after this she didn't believe him and asked others who told her the truth, with which she was greatly consoled (IC. V.1.10).

Once while in prayer I was shown quickly, without my seeing any form—but it was a totally clear representation—how all things are seen in God and how he holds them all in himself. How to put this in writing I don't know. But it was deeply impressed upon my soul, and it is one of the great favors the Lord has granted me and one of those that have most embarrassed me and made me ashamed when I recalled the sins I committed. I believe that had the Lord been pleased that I should have seen this before and that those who offend him should have seen it, neither I nor they would have had the heart or dared to offend him. I say "it seemed to me," without being able to affirm that I saw anything; but something must have been seen since I shall be able to draw a comparison. But the vision is seen in so subtle and delicate a manner that the intellect probably doesn't attain to it; or I don't know how to explain these visions that don't seem to be imaginative. Some of them must have something of the imaginative. But since the faculties are in rapture they are unable afterward to describe how the Lord is represented there and how he desires that they enjoy him.

Let us say, to make the comparison, that the Divinity is like a very clear diamond, much greater than all the world; or like a mirror, as I said referring to the soul in that other vision, except that it is a mirror in so sublime a way that I wouldn't know how to exaggerate this. And we could say that everything we do is visible in this diamond since it is of such a kind that it contains all things within itself; there is nothing that escapes its magnitude. It was a frightening experience for me to see in so short a time so many things joined together in this diamond, and it is most saddening, each time I recall, to see appearing in that pure brilliance things as ugly as were my sins. It happens that whenever I recall this, I fail to know how I can bear it; as a result I am then left with such shame that I don't think I know where to hide. Oh, who could explain this to those who commit very indecent and ugly sins, that they might recall that these sins are not hidden and that God is rightly aware of them since they take place squarely in the presence of the majesty? And we act so disrespectfully in front of him! I saw how truly hell is deserved through only one mortal sin because one cannot understand how dreadfully serious it is to commit this sin before such awesome majesty and how far from what he is are things of this sort. So his mercy is seen more clearly since even when we understand all this he bears with us (L. 40.9–10).

Pure Truth and Fount of all Truth

God as supreme truth, the measure and cause of everything that is, emerged as another exalted object of Teresa's contemplation. In order to describe this experience she had to speak in a more abstract manner than was her custom. In saying that God is true she meant that God is trustworthy. Truth is something reliable. God is worthy of trust, keeping his covenant of love forever with those who love him. Truth also denotes the plan and will of God. God's truth is his plan and will revealed in Scripture.

Once while in prayer the delight I felt within me was so great that, as someone who is unworthy of such good, I began to think about how I merited rather to be in that place I had seen was reserved for me in hell. For, as I said, I never forget the situation I there found myself in. With this reflection my soul began to grow more enkindled and there came upon me a spiritual rapture that I don't know how to describe. It seemed I was carried into and filled with that majesty I at other times understood. Within this majesty I was given knowledge of a truth that is the fulfillment of all truths. I don't know how to explain this because I didn't see anything. I was told without seeing anyone, but I clearly understood that it was Truth itself telling me: "This is no small thing I do for you, because it is one of the things for which you owe me a great deal; for all the harm that comes to the world comes from its not knowing the truths of Scripture in clarity and truth; not one iota of Scripture will fall short." To me it seemed I had always believed this, and that all the faithful believed it. He told me: "Alas, daughter, how few there are who truthfully love me! For if they loved me, I would reveal to them my secrets. Do you know what it is to love me truthfully? It is to understand that everything that is displeasing to me is a lie. By the beneficial effects this understanding will cause in your soul you shall see clearly what you now do not understand."

And this I have afterward come to realize, may the Lord be praised. For ever since then, that which I observe as not directed toward the service of God seems to me to be such vanity and deception that I wouldn't know how to describe the manner in which I understand this. Nor would I know how to describe the grief caused me by those who I see are in darkness about this truth, or, along with this, how to describe many other advantages that I shall mention here. The Lord spoke to me a particular word in this rapture by which he showed me extraordinary favor. I don't know how this came about, because I didn't see anything; but I was left with a feeling of indescribable good fortune and with the greatest and most authentic fortitude in using all my strength to carry out the least part of Sacred Scripture. It seems to me that no obstacle could cross my path that I wouldn't overcome.

From this divine Truth, which showed itself to me, there was engraved upon me, without my knowing how or what, a truth that gives me a new reverence toward God; for it gives knowledge of his majesty and power in an indescribable way: I know that this majesty and power are something great. There was left in me a keen desire to speak only those things that are very true, that reach beyond what is dealt with here in the world; and so I began to experience the pain of living in the world. This experience left me feeling great tenderness, consolation, and humility. I think that, without my understanding how, the Lord gave me very much with this favor. I felt no suspicion that it was an illusion. I didn't see anything, but I understood the great blessing there is in not paying attention to what doesn't bring us closer to God. Thus I understood that the Lord gave me understanding of what Truth itself is.

All I have mentioned I have come to know sometimes through locutions, at other times without them. Some things I understood more clearly than I understand what is told me in words. I understood extraordinary truths about this Truth, more than if many learned men had taught me. I don't think they could ever have impressed truth upon me in this way or made me understand so clearly the vanity of this world.

This truth, which I say was given to my understanding, is in itself truth, and it is without beginning or end; all other truths depend upon this truth, just as all other loves depend upon this love, and all other grandeurs upon this grandeur—although this statement is obscure if compared to the clear understanding the Lord wanted me to have. And what power this majesty appears to have since in so short a time he leaves such an abundant increase and things so marvelous impressed upon the soul! O my Grandeur and Majesty! What are you doing, my all-powerful Lord? Look upon whom you bestow such sovereign favors! Don't you recall that this soul has been an abyss of lies and a sea of vanities, and all through my own fault? For even though you gave me the natural temperament to abhor the lie, I myself in dealing with many things have lied. How do you bear it; my God? How is such great consolation and favor compatible with one who so poorly deserves this from you? (L. 40,1–4).

It also happens very quickly and ineffably that God will show within himself a truth that seems to leave in obscurity all those there are in creatures, and one understands very clearly that God alone is Truth, unable to lie. What David says in a psalm about every man being a liar is clearly understood. However frequently the verse may be heard, it is never understood as it is in this vision. God is everlasting Truth. I am reminded of Pilate, how he was often questioning our Lord when during the Passion he asked him, "What is truth?" and of the little we understand here below about this supreme Truth.

Once I was pondering why our Lord was so fond of this virtue of humility, and this thought came to me—in my opinion not as a result of reflection but suddenly: It is because God is supreme Truth; and to be humble is to walk in truth, for it is a very deep truth that of ourselves we have nothing good but only misery and nothingness. Whoever does not understand this walks in falsehood. The more anyone understands it the more she pleases the supreme Truth because she is walking in truth. Please God, sisters, we will be granted the favor never to leave this path of self-knowledge, amen (IC. VI. 10.5,7).

If it pains you not to see him with your bodily eyes, consider that seeing him so is not fitting for us. To see him in his glorified state is different from seeing him as he was when he walked through this world. On account of our natural weakness there is no person capable of enduring such a glorious sight, nor would anyone in the world want to continue in it. In seeing this Eternal Truth one would see that all the things we pay attention to here below are lies and jokes. And in beholding such great majesty, how would a little sinner like myself who has so much offended him remain so close to him (WP. 34.9)?

Chapter 8

Jesus Christ

Christ is the truth because he transmits the word and the revelation of the Father. Christ was the first supernatural reality that Teresa beheld. In explaining the stages of initial contemplation she speaks of its effects on both her faculties and spirit, of quiet and recollection, and so on. Then when Christ manifested his presence to her, she became aware in her mystical contemplation that he was the source of her contemplation and that he remained human, with a human body, as well as divine, that what could be said of his human nature could be predicated of him as God and that what could be said of his divine nature could be predicated of him as man.

Her christological contemplation taught her that God's mighty deeds of salvation were present among us through the humanity to which God was united in the Second Person of the Holy Trinity. She became thoroughly convinced that Christ's human nature, his humanity, is the instrument conjoined to God through which God saves us. She experienced Christ's company, that he wanted to be our companion and friend and walk with us as he did with his disciples. When he walked on this earth, he got hungry and thirsty, his feet got dirty from the dusty roads, he cried and laughed, and grew tired and slept. Through the earthly accounts of his life she was able to relate to him as though present, experience the power of his words and deeds as though these were directed to her. Through his earthly life, he became for her a model as well, especially in his suffering. In heaven, his humanity is so beautiful with such luminous splendor that, as earthly beings, we have little capacity for beholding the glory and majesty that is his. His glorified body itself has a purifying effect on Teresa. She frequently, then, refers to Jesus as His Majesty.

For Teresa, Christ is the fount and channel of every grace, the source of all our good. The coming of Jesus Christ shows how far the divine generosity can go. God gives his own Son. The source of this unheard of action is a mingling of tenderness, fidelity, mercy, and love. In this way God defines himself. For what the New Testament calls grace, Teresa will more often speak of in terms of God's favors or mercies toward her. The sensitivity of Jesus to human misery, his emotion in the presence of suffering, translates the tenderness and the mercy by which the God of the Old Testament is defined. Jesus Christ is grace, the gift of God which contains all other gifts. The grace of Christ radiates the generosity of the giver, enveloping at the same time with this generosity the creature who receives the gift. Finally, the abiding real presence of Christ in the Blessed Sacrament intensifies Teresa's experience of Christ as remaining close to her on this earth.

Human and Divine

After two years of all these prayers of mine and those of others offered for the said intention (that the Lord would either lead me by another way or make known the truth, for the locutions I mentioned that the Lord granted me were experienced very repeatedly), the following happened to me. Being in prayer on the feast day of the glorious Saint Peter, I saw or, to put it better, I felt Christ beside me; I saw nothing with my bodily eyes or with my soul, but it seemed to me that Christ was at my side—I saw that it was he, in my opinion, who was speaking to me. Since I was completely unaware that there could be a vision like this one, it greatly frightened me in the beginning; I did nothing but weep. However, by speaking one word alone to assure me, the Lord left me feeling as I usually did: quiet, favored, and without any fear. It seemed to me that Jesus Christ was always present at my side; but since this wasn't an imaginative vision, I didn't see any form. Yet I felt very clearly that he was always present at my right side and that he was the witness of everything I did. At no time in which I was a little recollected, or not greatly distracted, was I able to ignore that he was present at my side (L. 27.2).

It will happen while the soul is heedless of any thought about such a favor being granted to it, and though it never had a thought that it deserved this vision, that it will feel Jesus Christ, our Lord, beside it. Yet, it does not see him, either with the eyes of the body or with those of the soul. This is called an intellectual vision; I don't know why. I saw the person to whom God granted this favor, along with other favors I shall mention further on, quite worried in the beginning because since she didn't see anything she couldn't understand the nature of this vision. However, she knew so certainly that it was Jesus Christ, our Lord, who showed himself to her in that way that she couldn't doubt; I mean she couldn't doubt the vision was there. As to whether it was from God or not, even though she carried with her great effects to show that it was, she nonetheless was afraid. She had never heard of an intellectual vision, nor had she thought there was such a kind. But she understood very clearly that it was this same Lord who often spoke to her in the way mentioned. For until he granted her this favor I am referring to, she never knew who was speaking to her, although she understood the words.

I know that since she was afraid about this vision (for it isn't like the imaginative one that passes quickly, but lasts many days and sometimes even more than a year), she went very worried to her confessor. He asked her how since she didn't see anything she knew that it was our Lord; what kind of face he had. She told him she didn't know, that she didn't see any face, and that she couldn't say any more than what she had said, that what she did know was that he was the one who spoke to her and that the vision had not been fancied. And although some persons put many fears in her, she was still frequently unable to doubt, especially when the Lord said to her: "Do not be afraid, it is I." These words had so much power that from then on she could not doubt the vision, and she was left very much strengthened and happy over such good company. She saw clearly that the vision was a great help toward walking with a habitual remembrance of God and a deep concern about avoiding anything displeasing to him, for it seemed to her that he was always looking at her. And each time she wanted to speak with His Majesty in prayer, and even outside of it, she felt he was so near that he couldn't fail to hear her. But she didn't hear words spoken whenever she wanted; only unexpectedly when they were necessary. She felt he was walking at her right side, but she didn't experience this with those senses by which we can know that a person is beside us. This vision comes in another unexplainable, more delicate way. But it is so certain and leaves much certitude; even much more than the other visions do because in the visions that come through the senses one can be deceived, but not in the intellectual vision. For this latter brings great interior benefits and effects that couldn't be present if the experience were caused by melancholy; nor would the devil produce so much good; nor would the soul go about with such peace and continual desires to please God, and with so much contempt for everything that does not bring it to him. Afterward she understood clearly that the vision was not caused by the devil, which became more and more clear as time went on (IC. VI.8.2–3).

One day, while I was in prayer, the Lord desired to show me only his hands which were so very beautiful that I would be unable to exaggerate the beauty. This vision caused me great fear; any supernatural favor the Lord grants me frightens me at first, when it is new. After a few days I saw also that divine face which it seems left me completely absorbed. Since afterward he granted me the favor of seeing him entirely, I couldn't understand why the Lord showed himself to me in this way, little by little, until later I understood that His Majesty was leading me in accordance with my natural weakness. May he be blessed forever! So much glory would have been unbearable next to so lowly and wretched a subject as I; and as one who knew this, the merciful Lord was preparing me.

It will seem to your Reverence that strength like this wasn't necessary to see some hands and so beautiful a face. Glorified bodies have such beauty that the sight of so supernatural a beauty deriving from glory causes confusion. Thus the vision caused me a fear so great that I was completely agitated and disturbed, although afterward I remained so certain and secure and felt such other effects that I immediately lost the fear.

One feast day of Saint Paul, while I was at Mass, this most sacred humanity in its risen form was represented to me completely, as it is in paintings, with such wonderful beauty and majesty; I have written about it in particular to your Reverence when you insistently ordered me to do so. And writing about it was very difficult for me to do because one cannot describe this vision without ruining it. But as best I could I have already told you about it, and so there is no reason to speak of it here again. I only say that if there were nothing else to provide delight for one's vision in heaven than the exalted beauty of glorified bodies, this vision would be very great glory, especially the vision of the humanity of Jesus Christ, our Lord. And if even here on earth His Majesty shows himself according to what our wretchedness can bear, what will be the glory when such a blessing is enjoyed completely?

I never saw this vision—nor any other—with my bodily eyes, even though it is an imaginative one.

Those who know more about these matters than I say that the intellectual vision is more perfect than this one and that this one is much more perfect than visions seen with the bodily eyes. These latter, corporeal visions, they say, are the lowest and the kind in which the devil can cause more illusions; although at that time I couldn't understand this. But since an imaginative vision was being granted to me, I desired that I might see it with my bodily eyes so that my confessor wouldn't tell me that I had imagined it. And after the vision passed away, it also happened to me—and this was at once—that I thought that I had imagined it; thinking I had deceived my confessor, I was bothered about having told it to him. This was another cause for tears, and I went and explained to him. He asked me whether I had desired to deceive him. I told him the truth, for, in my opinion, I had not lied, nor had I intended to; nor for anything in the world would I say one thing for another. He well knew this, and so he tried to calm me. I felt so sorry for having gone to him with these things, for I don't know how the devil got me to torment myself with the thought that I had made up the vision.

But so quickly did the Lord grant me this favor and declare this truth that very soon the doubt about my imagining it left me, and afterward I saw clearly my foolishness. If I should have spent many years trying to imagine how to depict something so beautiful, I couldn't have, nor would I have known how to; it surpasses everything imaginable here on earth, even in just its whiteness and splendor (L. 28.1–4).

Well, let us say now that sometimes he wants to open the reliquary suddenly in order to do good to the one to whom he has lent it. Clearly, a person will afterward be much happier when she remembers the admirable splendor of the stone, and hence it will remain more deeply ingrained in her memory. So it happens here: when our Lord is pleased to give more delight to this soul, he shows it clearly his most sacred humanity in the way he desires; either as he was when he went about in the world or as he is after his resurrection. And even though the vision happens so quickly that we could compare it to a streak of lightning, this most glorious image remains so engraved on the imagination that I think it would be impossible to erase it until it is seen by the soul in that place where it will be enjoyed without end (IC. VI. 9.3).

To return, then, to what I was saying, since the Lord had begun to recall to me my wretched life and since I hadn't done anything, in my opinion, I wondered, in the midst of tears, if he desired to grant me some favor. It ordinarily happens when I receive some favor from the Lord that I am first humbled within myself so that I might see more clearly how far I am from deserving favors; I think the Lord must do this. After a short while my spirit was so enraptured it seemed to me to be almost entirely out of the body—at least the spirit isn't aware that it is living in the body. I saw the most sacred humanity with more extraordinary glory than I had ever seen. It was made manifest to me through a knowledge admirable and clear that the humanity was taken into the bosom of the Father. I wouldn't know how to describe the nature of this, because, without my seeing anything, it seemed to me I was in the presence of the Divinity. My amazement was such that I think for several days I couldn't return to myself; and it always seemed to me that I went about in the presence of that majesty of the Son of God, although the experience wasn't the same as when it first happened. This I understood clearly, but the vision is so strongly engraved on the imagination that no matter how short a while it lasts the impression left cannot be removed for some time; and the impression is very consoling and beneficial.

I saw this same vision three other times. It is in my opinion the most sublime vision the Lord granted me the favor of seeing, and it bears along with it marvelous benefits. It seems it purifies the soul in an extraordinary way and removes almost entirely the strength of this sensitive part of our nature. It is a great flame that seems to burn away and annihilate all of life's desires. For even though, glory to God, I didn't have any desires for vain things, it was made clear to me in this experience how everything was vanity. How vain, how truly vain are the lordships of earth! It is a powerful lesson for raising one's desires to pure truth. There is impressed upon one a reverence I wouldn't know how to speak of; for it is very different from the kind we can acquire here on earth. Great fear is caused in the soul when it sees how it dared, or how anyone can dare, to offend so extraordinary a majesty (L. 38.17).

Christ's Humanity, Fount and Channel of All Grace

I had no master and was reading these books in which I thought I was gradually coming to understand something. (And afterward I understood that if the Lord didn't show me, I was able to learn little from books, because there was nothing I understood until His Majesty gave me understanding through experience, nor did I know what I was doing.) As a result, when I began to experience something of supernatural prayer, I mean of the prayer of quiet, I strove to turn aside from everything corporeal, although I did not dare lift up the soul—since I was always so wretched, I saw that doing so would be boldness. But it seemed to me that I felt the presence of God, as was so, and I strove to recollect myself in his presence. This is a pleasing prayer, if God helps in it, and the delight is great. Since I felt that benefit and consolation, there was no one who could have made me return to the humanity of Christ; as a matter of fact, I thought the humanity was an impediment. O Lord of my soul and my Good, Jesus Christ crucified! At no time do I recall this opinion I had without feeling pain; it seems to me I became a dreadful traitor—although in ignorance.

I had been so devoted all my life to Christ (for I held this opinion toward the end, that is, just before the Lord granted me these favors of raptures and visions, and I didn't remain long in so extreme a practice of it); and thus I always returned to my custom of rejoicing in this Lord, especially when I received Communion. I wanted to keep ever before my eyes a painting or image of him since I was unable to keep him as engraved in my soul as I desired. Is it possible, my Lord, that it entered my mind for even an hour that you would be an impediment to my greater good? Where have all my blessings come from but from you? I don't want to think I was at fault in this, because it deeply saddens me—and certainly it was ignorance. Thus you desired, in your goodness, to remedy the matter by sending me someone who would draw me away from this error—and afterward by letting me see you so many times, as I shall explain later on—so that I would understand more clearly how great the error is, and tell many persons what I just said, and put it in writing here (L. 22.3.4).

If our nature or health doesn't allow us to think always about the Passion, since to do so would be arduous, who will prevent us from being with him in his risen state? We have him so near in the Blessed Sacrament, where he is already glorified and where we don't have to gaze upon him as being so tired and worn out, bleeding, wearied by his journeys, persecuted by those for whom he did so much good, and not believed in by the Apostles. Certainly there is no one who can endure thinking all the time about the many trials he suffered. Behold him here without suffering, full of glory, before ascending into heaven, strengthening some, encouraging others, our companion in the most Blessed Sacrament; it doesn't seem it was in his power to leave us for even a moment. And what a pity it was for me to have left you, my Lord, under the pretext of serving you more! When I was offending you I didn't know you; but how, once knowing you, did I think I could gain more by this path! Oh, what a bad road I was following, Lord! Now it seems to me I was walking on no path until you brought me back, for in seeing you at my side I saw all blessings. There was no trial that it wasn't good for me to suffer once I looked at you as you were, standing before the judges. Whoever lives in the presence of so good a friend and excellent a leader, who went ahead of us to be the first to suffer, can endure all things. The Lord helps us, strengthens us, and never fails; he is a true friend. And I see clearly, and I saw afterward, that God desires that if we are going to please him and receive his great favors, we must do so through the most sacred humanity of Christ, in whom he takes his delight. Many, many times have I perceived this truth through experience. The Lord has told it to me. I have definitely seen that we must enter by this gate if we desire His sovereign Majesty to show us great secrets.

Thus your Reverence and lordship should desire no other path even if you are at the summit of contemplation; on this road you walk safely. This Lord of ours is the one through whom all blessings come to us. He will teach us these things. In beholding his life we find that he is the best example. What more do we desire than to have such a good friend at our side, who will not abandon us in our labors and tribulations, as friends in the world do? Blessed are they who truly love him and always keep him at their side! Let us consider the glorious Saint Paul: it doesn't seem that any other name fell from his lips than that of Jesus as coming from one who kept the Lord close to his heart. Once I had come to understand this truth, I carefully considered the lives of some of the saints, the great contemplatives, and found that they hadn't taken any other path: Saint Francis demonstrates this through the stigmata; Saint Anthony of Padua, with the Infant; Saint Bernard found his delight in the humanity; Saint Catherine of Siena—and many others about whom your Reverence knows more than I (L. 22.6–7).

When God desires to suspend all the faculties, as we have seen in the kinds of prayer that were mentioned, it is clear that, even though we may not so desire, this presence is taken away. Then let it be so—gladly; blessed be such a loss that enables us to enjoy more that which it seems is lost. For then the soul is occupied completely in loving the One whom the intellect labored to know, and loves what it didn't understand, and rejoices in so great a joy that it couldn't have experienced it save by losing itself in order, as I say, to gain itself. But that we should skillfully and carefully accustom ourselves to avoid striving with all our strength to keep this most sacred humanity always present (and please the Lord it would be present always), this, I say, is what I don't think is good. The soul is left floating in the air, as they say; it seems it has no support no matter how much it may think it is full of God. It is an important thing that while we are living and are human we have human support. This disadvantage of not having human support leads to the other reason I referred to. With regard to the first reason, I already began to say that there is a small lack of humility in wanting to be Mary before having worked with Martha. When the Lord desires to raise up the soul, even if he does so from the first day, there is no reason for fear; but let us restrain ourselves as I believe I said before. This little speck of lack of humility, even though it seems to be nothing, does much harm to progress in contemplation (L. 22.9).

It will also seem to you that anyone who enjoys such lofty things will no longer meditate on the mysteries of the most sacred humanity of our Lord Jesus Christ. Such a person would now be engaged entirely in loving. This is a matter I wrote about at length elsewhere. They have contradicted me about it and said that I don't understand, because these are paths along which our Lord leads, and that when souls have already passed beyond the beginning stages it is better for them to deal with things concerning the divinity and flee from corporeal things. Nonetheless, they will not make me admit that such a road is a good one. Now it could be that I'm mistaken and that we are all saying the same thing. But I myself see that the devil tried to deceive me in this matter, and thus I have so learned my lesson from experience that I think, although I've spoken on this topic at other times, I will speak of it again here that you will proceed very carefully in this matter. And take notice that I dare say you should not believe anyone who tells you something else. I'll try to explain myself better than I did elsewhere. If anyone perhaps has written what a certain person told me, this would be good if the matter is explained at length, but to speak of it so summarily could do much harm to those of us who are not well informed.

It will also seem to some souls that they cannot think about the Passion, or still less about the Blessed Virgin and the lives of the saints; the remembrance of both of these latter is so very helpful and encouraging. I cannot imagine what such souls are thinking of. To be always withdrawn from corporeal things and enkindled in love is the trait of angelic spirits not of those who live in mortal bodies. It's necessary that we speak to, think about, and become the companions of those who having had a mortal body accomplished such great feats for God. How much more is it necessary not to withdraw through one's own efforts from all our good and help which is the most sacred humanity of our Lord Jesus Christ. I cannot believe that these souls do so, but they just don't understand; and they will do harm to themselves and to others. At least I assure them that they will not enter these last two dwelling places. For if they lose the guide, who is the good Jesus, they will not hit upon the right road. It will be quite an accomplishment if they remain safely in the other dwelling places. The Lord himself says that he is the way; the Lord says also that he is the light and that no one can go to the Father but through him, and "anyone who sees me sees my Father" [Jn. 8:12; 14:6,9]. They will say that another meaning is given to these words. I don't know about those other meanings; I have got along very well with this one that my soul always feels to be true.

There are some souls—and there are many who have spoken about it to me—who brought by our Lord to perfect contemplation would like to be in that prayer always; but that is impossible. Yet this favor of the Lord remains with them in such a way that afterward they cannot engage as before in discursive thought about the mysteries of the Passion and life of Christ. I don't know the reason, but this inability is very common, for the intellect becomes less capable of meditation. I believe the reason must be that since in meditation the whole effort consists in seeking God and that once God is found the soul becomes used to seeking him again through the work of the will, the soul doesn't want to tire itself by working with the intellect. Likewise, it seems to me that since this generous faculty, which is the will, is already enkindled, it wants to avoid, if it can, using the other faculty; and it doesn't go wrong. But to avoid this will be impossible, especially before the soul reaches these last two dwelling places; and the soul will lose time, for the will often needs the help of the intellect so as to be enkindled (IC. VI.7.5–7).

At this point, someone may respond that he cannot dwell on these things, and, because of what was said, perhaps he will in a certain way be right. You already know that discursive thinking with the intellect is one thing and representing truths to the intellect by means of the memory is another. You may say, perhaps, that you do not understand me, and indeed it could be that I don't know how to explain the matter; but I shall do the best I can. By meditation I mean much discursive reflection with the intellect in the following way: we begin to think about the favor God granted us in giving us his only Son, and we do not stop there, but go on to the mysteries of his whole glorious life; or we begin to think about the prayer in the garden, but the intellect doesn't stop until he is on the cross; or we take a phase of the Passion like, let us say, the arrest, and we proceed with this mystery considering in detail the things there are to think of and feel about the betrayal of Judas, the flight of the apostles, and all the rest; this kind of reflection is an admirable and very meritorious prayer.

This prayer is the kind that those whom God has brought to supernatural things and to perfect contemplation are right in saying they cannot practice. As I have said, I don't know the reason, but usually they cannot practice discursive reflection. But I say that a person will not be right if he says he does not dwell on these mysteries or often have them in mind, especially when the Catholic Church celebrates them. Nor is it possible for the soul to forget that it has received so much from God, so many precious signs of love, for these are living sparks that will enkindle it more in its love for our Lord. But I say this person doesn't understand himself, because the soul understands these mysteries in a more perfect manner. The intellect represents them in such a way, and they are so stamped on the memory, that the mere sight of the Lord fallen to the ground in the garden with that frightful sweat is enough to last the intellect not only an hour but many days, while it looks with a simple gaze at who he is and how ungrateful we have been for so much suffering. Soon the will responds even though it may not do so with tender feelings, with the desire to serve somehow for such a great favor and to suffer something for one who suffered so much, and with other similar desires relating to what the memory and intellect are dwelling upon. I believe that for this reason a person cannot go on to further discursive reflection on the Passion, and this inability makes persons think that they cannot think about it.

If they don't dwell on these mysteries in the way that was mentioned, it is good that they strive to do so, for I know that doing so will not impede the most sublime prayer. I don't think it's good to fail to dwell often on these mysteries. If as a result the Lord suspends the intellect, well and good; for even though the soul may not so desire he will make it abandon what it was dwelling on. And I am very certain that this procedure is not a hindrance but a very great help toward every good; the hindrance would come from a great deal of work with the discursive reflection I mentioned in the beginning. I hold that one who has advanced further along cannot practice this discursive reflection. It could be that one can, for God leads souls by many paths. But let not those who can travel by the road of discursive thought condemn those who cannot, or judge them incapable of enjoying the sublime blessings that lie enclosed in the mysteries of our good, Jesus Christ. Nor will anyone make me think, however spiritual he may be, that he will advance by trying to turn away from these mysteries (IC. VI.7.10–12).

Christ the Life of the Soul

And that its life is Christ is understood better, with the passing of time, by the effects this life has. Through some secret aspirations the soul understands clearly that it is God who gives life to our soul. These aspirations come very, very often in such a living way that they can in no way be doubted. The soul feels them very clearly even though they are indescribable. But the feeling is so powerful that sometimes the soul cannot avoid the loving expressions they cause, such as: O Life of my life! Sustenance that sustains me! and things of this sort. For from those divine breasts where it seems God is always sustaining the soul there flow streams of milk bringing comfort to all the people of the castle. It seems the Lord desires that in some manner these others in the castle may enjoy the great deal the soul is enjoying and that from that full-flowing river, where this tiny fount is swallowed up, a spurt of that water will sometimes be directed toward the sustenance of those who in corporeal things must serve these two who are wed. Just as a distracted person would feel this water if suddenly bathed in it, and would be unable to avoid feeling it, so are these operations recognized, and even with greater certitude. For just as a great gush of water could not reach us if it didn't have a source, as I have said, so it is understood clearly that there is Someone in the interior depths who shoots these arrows and gives life to this life, and that there is a Sun in the interior of the soul from which a brilliant light proceeds and is sent to the faculties. The soul, as I have said, does not move from that center nor is its peace lost; for the very One who gave peace to the apostles when they were together can give it to the soul (IC. VII.2.6).

Chapter 9

The Indwelling of the Blessed Trinity

Jesus Christ brought Teresa into the innermost place in her soul where the scales fell from her eyes and she beheld in God the three Persons of the Holy Trinity who although one God communicate with each other, love each other, and know each other. She saw that all three, through their reciprocal interrelationship, constitute "the same Being, the same Life, the same God." And she in turn could know and love and communicate with each of them. They became in the one God her habitual companions; their presence was manifested to her.

One day, after the feast of Saint Matthew, being in the state I'm usually in since I've seen the vision of the Blessed Trinity and how it dwells in a soul in the state of grace, a very clear understanding of this mystery was granted to me so that in certain ways and through comparisons I beheld it in an imaginative vision. Although at other times knowledge of the Blessed Trinity was given me through an intellectual vision, the truth, after a few days, no longer remained with me so that I could think about it and find consolation in it, as I can now. And now I realize that in a similar way I had heard about this truth from learned men but didn't understand it as I do at present, although I always believed it without hesitation because I have never had temptations against the faith.

To us ignorant people it appears that all three Persons of the Blessed Trinity are—as represented in paintings—in one Person, as when three faces are painted on one body. And thus we are so scared away that it seems the mystery is impossible and that no one should desire to think about it. For the intellect feels hindered and fears lest it might have doubts about this truth, and it thereby loses something very beneficial.

What was represented to me were three distinct Persons, for we can behold and speak to each one. Afterward I reflected that only the Son took human flesh, through which this truth of the Trinity was seen. These Persons love, communicate with, and know each other. Well, if each one is by himself, how is it that we say all three are one essence, and believe it? And this is a very great truth for which I would die a thousand deaths. In all three Persons there is no more than one will, one power, and one dominion, in such a way that one cannot do anything without the others. But no matter how many creatures there are, there is only one Creator. Could the Son create an ant without the Father? No, for it is all one power, and the same goes for the Holy Spirit; thus there is only one all-powerful God and all three Persons are one majesty. Could one love the Father without loving the Son and the Holy Spirit? No, but anyone who pleases one of these three Persons, pleases all three, and the same goes for anyone who might offend one. Could the Father exist without the Son or without the Holy Spirit? No, because the essence is one; and where one is, all three are, for they cannot be separated. Well, how do we see that the three Persons are separate, and how did the Son take on human flesh and not the Father or the Holy Spirit? This I haven't understood. The theologians know. I know well that in that work so marvelous all three were present, and I don't get involved in thinking a lot about this. I immediately conclude my reflection with the observation that God is all-powerful and that whatever he wanted to do he did, and thus he will be able to do all he desires. And when I understand less, I believe more; and this belief gives me greater devotion. May he be blessed forever. Amen (ST. 29).

I have experienced this presence of the three Persons, which I mentioned at the beginning, up to this day which is the feast of the Commemoration of Saint Paul. They are very habitually present in my soul. Since I was accustomed to experience only the presence of Jesus, it always seemed to me there was some obstacle to my seeing three Persons, although I understand there is only one God. And the Lord told me today while I was reflecting upon this that I was mistaken in thinking of things of the soul through comparison with corporeal things, that I should know that these spiritual things are very different and that the soul is capable of great rejoicing. It seemed to me there came the thought of how a sponge absorbs and is saturated with water; so, I thought, was my soul which was overflowing with that divinity and in a certain way rejoicing within itself and possessing the three Persons.

I also heard the words: "Don't try to hold me within yourself, but try to hold yourself within me." It seemed to me that from within my soul—where I saw these three Persons present— these Persons were communicating themselves to all creation without fail, nor did they fail to be with me (ST. 14).

In this seventh dwelling place the union comes about in a different way: our good God now desires to remove the scales from the soul's eyes and let it see and understand, although in a strange way, something of the favor he grants it. . . . First there comes an enkindling in the spirit in the manner of a cloud of magnificent splendor; and these Persons are distinct, and through an admirable knowledge the soul understands as a most profound truth that all three Persons are one substance and one power and one knowledge and one God alone. It knows in such a way that what we hold by faith, it understands, we can say, through sight—although the sight is not with the bodily eyes nor with the eyes of the soul, because we are not dealing with an imaginative vision. . . . In the extreme interior, in some place very deep within itself, the nature of which it doesn't know how to explain, because of a lack of learning, it perceives this divine company.

You may think that as a result the soul will be outside itself and so absorbed that it will be unable to be occupied with anything else. On the contrary, the soul is much more occupied than before with everything pertaining to the service of God; and once its duties are over it remains with that enjoyable company. If the soul does not fail God, he will never fail, in my opinion, to make his presence clearly known to it. It has strong confidence that since God has granted this favor he will not allow it to lose the favor. Though the soul thinks this, it goes about with greater care than ever not to displease him in anything (IC. VII.1.6–8).

Chapter 10

The Power of God's Words

God spoke to Teresa in a variety of ways which she carefully analyzed. She experienced one of the most characteristic traits of the living God: God speaks to human beings. But the significant object of her experience was the power of God's word. God's word is not only a message but a dynamic reality, a power that brings about the effects at which God aims.

While in this great affliction then (although at that time I had not begun to have any vision), these words alone were enough to take it away and bring me complete quiet: "Do not fear, daughter; for I am, and I will not abandon you; do not fear." It seems to me that from the way I felt many hours would have been necessary and no one would have been able to persuade me to be at peace. And behold by these words alone I was given calm together with fortitude, courage, security, quietude, and light so that in one moment I saw my soul become another. It seems to me I would have disputed with the entire world that these words came from God. Oh, what a good God! Oh, how good a Lord and how powerful! He provides not only the counsel but also the remedy! His words are works! Oh, God help me; and how he strengthens faith and increases love!

Hence it is, indeed, that I often recalled the time the Lord commanded the winds to be quiet when the storm arose at sea, and so I said: Who is this that all my faculties obey him thus, who gives in a moment and in the midst of such great darkness, who softens a heart that seemed like stone, and who gives the water of gentle tears where it seemed there would be dryness for a long time? Who imparts these desires? Who bestows this courage? For it occurred to me to think: What do I fear? What is this? I desire to serve this Lord; I aim for nothing else but to please him. I want no happiness, no rest, no other good but to do his will (for I felt deeply certain in my opinion that I could make this assertion). If this Lord is powerful, as I see that he is and I know that he is, and if the devils are his slaves (and there is no doubt about this because it's a matter of faith), what evil can they do to me since I am a servant of this Lord and King? Why shouldn't I have the fortitude to engage in combat with all of hell? (L. 25.18).

It happened to me at other times that I was suffering great tribulations and criticism, on account of a certain matter I shall speak of afterward, from almost the entire city where I live and from my order, and afflicted by the many occasions there were for becoming disturbed, when the Lord said to me: "Why are you afraid? Do you not know that I am all-powerful? I will fulfill what I have promised." (And it was truly fulfilled later.) I was immediately left with such fortitude that it seemed to me I would again undertake other things, even though they would cost me greater trials, and I would once more take suffering upon myself in order to serve him. This has happened so many times that I wouldn't be able to count them. Often his words to me were rebukes—and still are when I commit imperfections. These rebukes are enough to dissolve a soul; at least they bear amendment with them, because His Majesty, as I said, gives both the counsel and the cure. At other times the locutions bring my past sins to mind—especially when the Lord wants to grant me some exceptional favor; it seems the soul is already before the true Judge since they represent the truth to it with such clear understanding that it doesn't know where to hide. At other times the Lord warns me of some dangers I'm in, or of other persons, and about things of the future—three of four years in advance very often—all of which have been fulfilled. Some of these can be pointed out concretely. Thus there are so many reasons for knowing that the words come from God that in my opinion one cannot be ignorant of this (L. 26.2).

Chapter 11

The Word of God in Scripture

Teresa frequently experienced the revealed word through select bits of Scripture that disclosed their substance in the light of her contemplation. She became clearly aware that there is a secret way of understanding the revealed word; that is, through interior experience. Most often the divine locutions received by Teresa were taken from Scripture or given through close equivalents.

And, in fact, it has happened to me that while in this quietude, and understanding hardly anything of the Latin prayers, especially of the psalter, I have not only understood how to render the Latin verse in the vernacular but have gone beyond to rejoicing in the meaning of the verse (L. 15.8).

For a number of years now the Lord has given me great delight each time I hear or read some words from Solomon's "Song of Songs." The delight is so great that without understanding the vernacular meaning of the Latin my soul is stirred and recollected more than by devotional books written in the language I understand. And this happens almost all the time, and even when the Latin words were translated for me into the vernacular I did not understand the text any more (M. Pro.1)

I know someone who for a number of years had many fears, and nothing gave her assurance, but the Lord was pleased that she hear some words from the "Song of Songs," and through them she understood that her soul was being well guided. As I have said, she understood that it was possible for a soul in love with its Spouse to experience all these favors, swoons, deaths, afflictions, delights, and joys in relation to him. It does so after it has left all the world's joys out of love for him and is completely given over and abandoned into his hands, and when it has done this not just in words, as happens with some, but in all truth, confirmed with works (M. 1.6).

Before I go any further, and so as not to forget, I want to say one thing—very important in my opinion—although the matter would fit better at another time. I hold as certain that there are many persons who approach the most Blessed Sacrament (and please the Lord I be lying) with serious mortal sins. Yet, if such persons were to hear a soul dying with love of its God say these words ["Let him kiss me with the kiss of his mouth," Sg. 1:9], they would be surprised and consider it great boldness. At least I am sure they themselves would not say them, for these words and others similar ones in the "Song of Songs" are said by love. Since such persons have no love, they can easily read the "Song of Songs" every day and not themselves become involved with the words; nor would they even dare take the words on their lips. For truly even hearing them makes one fear, for these words bear in themselves great majesty. How much majesty you bear, my Lord, in the most Blessed Sacrament. But since these persons do not have a living faith but a dead one, you do not speak to them when they see you so humble under the species of bread. They do not deserve to hear—and thus they are not so daring (M.1.11).

God's Word in Times of Crisis

This frightened and pained me so much that I didn't know what to do; I was all tears. And while in an oratory very much afflicted, not knowing what would become of me, I read in a book—which it seems the Lord placed in my hands—what Saint Paul said, that God was very faithful, that he would never let those who love him be deceived by the devil [1 Cor 10:13]. This consoled me very deeply (L. 23.15).

When they forbade the reading of many books in the vernacular, I felt that prohibition very much because reading some of them was an enjoyment for me, and I could no longer do so since only the Latin editions were allowed. The Lord said to me: "Don't be sad, for I shall give you a living book." I was unable to understand why this was said to me, since I had not yet experienced any visions. Afterward, within only a few days, I understood very clearly, because I received so much to think about and such recollection in the presence of what I saw, and the Lord showed so much love for me by teaching me in many ways, that I had very little or almost no need for books. His Majesty had become the true book in which I saw the truths. Blessed be such a book that leaves what must be read and done so impressed that you cannot forget (L. 26.5)!

At other times, by one word the Lord spoke to me. Only by his saying, "Don't grow weary, don't be afraid," as I've already mentioned elsewhere. I was left completely cured (L. 30.14).

What he said grieved me more than everything else put together, since it seemed to me that if I had been an occasion or had been at fault for some offense against God, and that if these visions had been an illusion, all the prayer I had experienced was self-deception, and that I was being misled and going astray. This made me so extremely distressed I was thrown into complete confusion and severely afflicted. But the Lord, who never failed me, who in all these trials I enumerated often consoled and fortified me—there is no reason to mention it all specifically here—then told me not to be anxious; that I had served God a great deal and had not offended him in that project; that I should do what my confessor ordered me to do by being silent for the present, until it would come time to return to the task. I was left so consoled and happy that the persecution hanging over me seemed to be all nothing (L. 33.3).

And while I was feeling really desolate, the Lord said to me: "Don't you know that I am mighty? What do you fear?" And he assured me the new monastery would not be suppressed. As a result I was left very consoled (L. 36.16).

When this favor is granted them in secret, their esteem for it is great; when it is given in the presence of other persons, their embarrassment and shame are so strong that the pain and worry over what those who saw it will think somehow take the soul away from what was being enjoyed. For these persons know the malice of the world, and they understand that the world will not perhaps regard the experience for what it is, but that what the Lord should be praised for will perhaps be the occasion for rash judgments. In some ways it seems to me that this pain and embarrassment amount to a lack of humility, for if this person desires to be reviled, what difference does it make what others think? But the soul cannot control such feelings. One who was in this affliction heard from the Lord: "Don't be afflicted, either they will praise me or criticize you; and in either case you gain." I learned afterward that this person was very much consoled and encouraged by these words, and I put them down here in case one of you might find herself in this affliction (IC. VI. 4.16).

Returning, then, to the first of the different kinds of locutions; whether or not the words come from the interior part of the soul, from the superior part, or from the exterior part doesn't matter in discerning whether or not they are from God. The surest signs they are from God that can be had, in my opinion, are these: the first and truest is the power and authority they bear, for locutions from God effect what they say. Let me explain myself better. A soul finds itself in the midst of all the tribulation and disturbance that was mentioned, in darkness of the intellect and in dryness; with one word alone of these locutions from the Lord ("don't be distressed"), it is left calm and free from all distress, with great light, and without all that suffering in which it seemed to it that all the learned men and all who might come together to give it reasons for not being distressed would be unable to remove its affliction no matter how hard they tried. Or, it is afflicted because its confessor and others have told it that its spirit is from the devil, and it is all full of fear; with one word alone ("it is I, fear not"), the fear is taken way completely, and the soul is most comforted, thinking that nothing would be sufficient to make it believe anything else. Or, it is greatly distressed over how certain serious business matters will turn out; it hears that it should be calm, that everything will turn out all right. It is left certain and free of anxiety. And this is the way in many other instances (IC. VI.3.5).

And although some persons put many fears in her, she was still frequently unable to doubt, especially when the Lord said to her: "Do not be afraid, it is I." These words had so much power that from then on she could not doubt the vision, and she was left very much strengthened and happy over such good company (IC. VI.8.3).

God's Word and the Mystical Union

Perhaps this is what Saint Paul means in saying "He that is joined or united to the Lord becomes one spirit with him" [1 Cor. 6:17], and is referring to this sovereign marriage, presupposing that His Majesty has brought the soul to it through union. And he also says: "For me to live is Christ, and to die is gain" [Phil. 1:21]. The soul as well, I think, can say these words now because this state is the place where the little butterfly we mentioned dies, and with the greatest joy because its life is now Christ (IC. VII.2.5).

Who would have claimed I would so quickly fall after so many gifts from God, after His Majesty had begun to give me virtues which themselves roused me to his service, after I had seen myself almost dead and in such serious danger of being condemned, after having been raised up body and soul so that all who saw me were amazed to see me alive! What is this, my Lord! Must we live in so dangerous a life? For in writing this it seems to me that with your favor and through your mercy I can say what Saint Paul said, although not with such perfection, that I no longer live but that you, my Creator, live in me [cf. Gal. 2:20]. The reason is that for some years now, insofar as I can understand, you have held me by your hand, and I see in myself desires and resolutions—and in some way have received proof of them through experience with many things during these years—not to do anything against your will no matter how small; although I must offend Your Majesty in many ways without knowing it (L. 6.9).

Well once this silkworm is grown—in the beginning I dealt with its growth—it begins to spin the silk and build the house wherein it will die. I would like to point out here that this house is Christ. Somewhere, it seems to me, I have read or heard that our life is hidden in Christ or in God (both are the same), or that our life is Christ [Col. 3:3–4]. Whether the quotation is exact or not doesn't matter for what I intend (IC. V.2.4).

God's Word in the Straits of Ecstasy

This pain and glory joined together left me confused; I couldn't understand how such a combination was possible. Oh, what it is to see a wounded soul! I say that this reality should be understood in such a way that the soul is said to be wounded for a very sublime reason and there be clear awareness that the soul did not cause this love, but that seemingly a spark from the very great love the Lord has for it suddenly fell upon it, making it burn all over. Oh, how many times when I am in this state do I recall that verse of David: *Quemadmodum desiderat cervus ad fontes aquarum* [As the deer longs for the fountains of water (Ps. 42:2)];

for it seems to me that I experience it literally within myself (L. 29.11).

Oh, how painful it is for a soul who finds itself in this stage to have to return to dealing with everything, to behold and see the face of this so poorly harmonized life, to waste time in taking care of bodily needs, sleeping, and eating! Everything wearies it; it doesn't know how to flee; it sees itself captured and in chains. Then it feels more truly the misery of life and the captivity we endure because of our bodies. It knows the reason Saint Paul had for beseeching God to be liberated from the body [Rom. 7:24]; it cries out with him; it begs God for freedom, as I have mentioned at other times. But in this state the impulse is often so great that it seems the soul wants to leave the body and go in search of this freedom since there is no one else who will free it. It goes about as one sold into a foreign land, and what wearies it most is that it doesn't find many who will complain with it and beg for this freedom; rather, what is more common is the desire to live. Oh, if only we were not bound to anything, if our satisfaction were not derived from any earthly thing, how the pain experienced from always living without him and the desire to enjoy the true life would temper the fear of death! (L. 21.6).

With this communication the desire increases and also the extreme sense of solitude in which, even though the soul is in that desert, it sees with a pain so delicate and penetrating that it can, I think literally say: *Vigilavi, et factus sum sicut passer solitarius in tecto* [I have watched and become as a sparrow all alone on the housetop (Ps. 102:8)]. (And perhaps the royal prophet said it while being in the same solitude, although since he was a saint the Lord would have given him this experience in a more intense way.) Hence this verse then came to mind, for I think I saw it realized in myself. It consoled me to know that other persons—and such great ones—had experienced so extreme a solitude. Thus it seems that the soul is not in itself, but on the roof or housetop of itself and of all created things because it seems to me to be even above the very superior part of the soul.

At other times it seems the soul goes about as though compelled to say and ask itself: "where is your God?" [Ps. 42:4] It is interesting to note that I didn't know what the vernacular of this verse was; after I understood it, I was consoled to see that the Lord had brought it to my mind without my having played any part in the matter. At other times I recalled what Saint Paul says, that he is crucified to the world [Gal. 6:14]. I am not saying that these words apply here; I realize they don't. But it seems to me that the soul is crucified since no consolation comes to it from heaven, nor is it in heaven; neither does it desire any from earth, nor is it on earth. Receiving no help from either side, it is as though crucified between heaven and earth. That which comes from heaven (which, as I said, is so admirable a knowledge of God, very far above every desirable thing) causes more torment because the desire increases in such a way that, in my opinion, the intense pain sometimes takes away sensory consciousness; but this intensity lasts only a short time. The experience resembles the death agony with the difference that the suffering bears along with it such great happiness that I don't know what to compare it to. It is an arduous delightful martyrdom since it admits no earthly thing representable to the soul, even if this be what is usually more pleasing to it. The soul, it seems, immediately hurls such things from itself. It clearly understands that it desires only its God. It doesn't love any particular aspect of him, but loves him all together and knows not what it loves. I say it "knows not" because the imagination doesn't represent anything; nor, in my opinion, do the faculties function during much of the time that this takes place. Just as it is joy that suspends the faculties in union and rapture, so it is pain that suspends them here (L. 20.10–11).

You will tell me that this feeling is an imperfection and ask why the soul doesn't conform to the will of God since it is so surrendered to him. Until now it could do this, and has spent its life doing so. As for now, the reasoning faculty is in such a condition that the soul is not the master of it, nor can the soul think of anything else than of why it is grieving, of how it is absent from

its Good, and of why it should want to live. It feels a strange solitude because no creature in all the earth provides it company, nor
do I believe would any heavenly creature, not being the One
whom it loves; rather, everything torments it. But the soul sees
that it is like a person hanging, who cannot support himself on
any earthly thing; nor can it ascend to heaven. On fire with this
thirst, it cannot get to the water; and the thirst is not one that is
endurable but already at such a point that nothing will take it
away. Nor does the soul desire that the thirst be taken away save
by that water of which our Lord spoke to the Samaritan woman
[Jn. 4:7–14]. Yet no one gives such water to the soul (IC. VI.11.5).

The soul sees such great blindness in pleasures and how with
them one buys trouble—even for this life—and worry. What
restlessness! What little happiness! What vain labor! In this
prayer it sees not only serious faults and cobwebs in its soul but
any speck of dust no matter how small because the sun is very
bright. And so, no matter how much a soul labors to become
perfect, if this sun truly takes hold of it, everything is seen as very
turbid. The soul is like water in a glass: the water looks very clear
if the sun doesn't shine on it; but when the sun shines on it, it
seems to be full of dust particles. This comparison is an exact one.
Before being in this ecstasy the soul thinks it is careful about not
offending God and that it is doing what it can in conformity with
its strength. But once it is brought into prayer, which this sun of
justice bestows on it and which opens its eyes, it sees so many
dust particles that it would want to close its eyes again. It is not
yet so much a child of this powerful eagle that it can gaze steadily
at this sun. But for the little time that it holds its eyes open, it sees
that it is itself filled with mud. It recalls the psalm that says: Who
will be just in your presence? [Ps. 143:2] (L. 20.28).

God's Word and the Indwelling

On the Tuesday following Ascension Thursday, having
remained a while in prayer after Communion, I was grieved

because I was so distracted I couldn't concentrate. So I complained to the Lord about our miserable nature. My soul began to enkindle, and it seemed to me I knew clearly in an intellectual vision that the entire Blessed Trinity was present. In this state my soul understood by a certain kind of representation (like an illustration of the truth), in such a way that my dullness could perceive, how God is three and one. And so it seemed that all three Persons were represented distinctly in my soul and they spoke to me, telling me that from this day I would see an improvement in myself in respect to three things and that each one of these Persons would grant me a favor: one, the favor of charity; another, the favor of being able to suffer gladly; and the third, the favor of experiencing this charity with an enkindling in the soul. I understood those words the Lord spoke, that the three divine Persons would be with the soul in grace [Jn. 14:23]; for I saw them within myself in the way described (ST. 13.1).

The presence of the three Persons is so impossible to doubt that it seems one experiences what Saint John says, that they will make their abode in the soul [Jn. 14:23] (ST. 65.9).

Here all three Persons communicate themselves to it, speak to it, and explain those words of the Lord in the gospel: that he and the Father and the Holy Spirit will come to dwell with the soul that loves him and keeps his commandments [Jn. 14:23] (IC. VII.1.6).

God's Word in the Peace of the Soul's Center

This you will have experienced, sisters. For I think that when one has reached the prayer of union the Lord goes about with this concern if we do not grow negligent in keeping his commandments. When this impulse comes to you, remember that it comes from this interior dwelling place where God is in our soul, and praise him very much. For certainly that note or letter is his, written with intense love and in such a way that he wants you alone to understand it and what he asks of you in it. By no means should you fail to respond to His Majesty, even though you may be externally occupied or in conversation with some persons. For it will often happen that our Lord will want to grant you this secret favor in public, and it is very easy—since the response is interior—to do what I'm saying and make an act of love, or say what Saint Paul said: "Lord, what will you have me do?" [Acts 9:6]. In many ways he will teach you there what will be pleasing to him and the acceptable time. I think it is understood that he hears us, and this touch, which is so delicate, almost always disposes the soul to be able to do what was said with a resolute will (IC. VII.3.9).

Every way in which the Lord helps the soul here, and all he teaches it, takes place with such quiet and so noiselessly that, seemingly to me, the work resembles the building of Solomon's temple where no sound was heard [1 Kgs. 6:7]. So in this temple of God, in this his dwelling place, he alone and the soul rejoice together in the deepest silence. There is no reason for the intellect to stir or seek anything, for the Lord who created it wishes to give it repose here and that through a small crevice it might observe what is taking place. At times this sight is lost and the other faculties do not allow the intellect to look, but this happens for only a very short time. In my opinion, the faculties are not lost here; they do not work, but remain as though in amazement (IC. VII.3.11).

Chapter 12

The Church on Earth a Pilgrim People

Another object Teresa attained in her contemplation was the mystery of the Church. She perceived an unfathomable identity between Christ and the Church and all that accompanies this. The Church is united to Christ as her principle of life, cohesion, and growth. Communion with Jesus Christ brings about a communion among Christians. In this communion they share the word of the apostles, which engenders faith in Jesus resurrected, Lord and Christ, leader and savior. They share in the Eucharist, and in prayer together. The members are grouped under the authority of the successors of the apostles. This leadership, a charism of the Holy Spirit, has a building and unifying role. The Church must guard and defend the deposit of sound instruction received from the apostles. The power to protect this treasure of faith is the power to enunciate and make it explicit without error.

But the pilgrim Church here on earth has not found unity to come easily. Teresa was greatly afflicted by the breakup of unity within the Church in her time. For this work of promoting unity she was strongly aware of the importance of learning. Theologians and preachers have the heavy task of enlightening and defending the Church. Such work along with a fervent love among the faithful would provide the remedy for the Church's divisions.

She was convinced that force, violence, religious wars would only wreak more havoc and accomplish no good. What she and her nuns could do was plead through their lives of prayer for the Church and its theologians and leaders, always seeking to increase in fervent love. Then through their close union with Christ, their prayers would be fruitful in accord with her Lord's promise.

At that time news reached me of the harm being done in France. The news distressed me greatly, and, as though I could do something or were something, I wept with the Lord and begged him that I might remedy so much evil. It seemed to me that I would have given a thousand lives to save one soul out of the many that were being lost there. All my longing was and still is that since he has so many enemies and so few friends that these few friends be good ones. As a result I resolved to do the little that was in my power; that is, to follow the evangelical counsels as perfectly as I could and strive that these few persons who live here do the same. I did this trusting in the great goodness of God, who never fails to help anyone who is determined to give up everything for him. My trust was that if these sisters matched the ideal my desires had set for them, my faults would not have much strength in the midst of so many virtues; and I could thereby please the Lord in some way. Since we would all be occupied in prayer for those who are the defenders of the Church and for preachers and for learned men who protect her from attack, we could help as much as possible this Lord of mine who is so roughly treated by those for whom he has done so much good (W. 1.2).

The world is all in flames; they want to sentence Christ again, so to speak, since they raise a thousand false witnesses against him; they want to ravage his Church—and are we to waste time asking for things that if God were to give them we'd have one soul less in heaven? No, my sisters, this is not the time to be discussing with God matters that have little importance (W. 1.5).

Human forces are not sufficient to stop the spread of this fire caused by these heretics, even though people have tried to see if with the force of arms they could remedy all the evil that is making such progress. It has seemed to me that what is necessary is a different approach, the approach of a lord when in time of war his land is overrun with enemies and he finds himself restricted on all sides. He withdraws to a city that he has well fortified and from there sometimes strikes his foe. Those who are in the city, being chosen people, are such that they can do more by themselves than many cowardly soldiers can. And often victory is won in this way. At least, even though victory is not won, these chosen people are not conquered. For since they have no traitor, they cannot be conquered—unless through starvation. In this example the starvation cannot be such as to force them to surrender—to die, yes; but not to surrender.

But why have I said this? So that you understand, my sisters, that what we must ask God is that in this little castle where there are already good Christians not one of us will go over to the enemy and that God will make the captains of this castle or city, who are the preachers and theologians, very advanced in the way of the Lord. Since most of them belong to religious orders, ask God that they advance very far in the perfection of religious life and their vocation; this is most necessary. For as I have said, it is the ecclesiastical, not the secular, arm that will save us. Since in neither the ecclesiastical nor the secular arm can we be of any help to our king, let us strive to be the kind of persons whose prayers can be useful in helping those servants of God who through much toil have strengthened themselves with learning and a good life and have labored so as now to help the Lord (W. 3.1–2).

I feel in me the greatest desire, more than usual, that God have persons, especially learned men, who serve him with complete detachment and who are held back by nothing here below; because I see it is all a mockery. Since I'm aware of the great needs of the Church—for these afflict me so much that it seems to me too silly to feel sorrow about anything else—I don't do anything but pray to God for these persons. For I see that one person who is completely perfect would do more good with a true, fervent love of God than many others would with luke-warmness (ST. 3.7).

It sometimes happened to me—and even now it does, although not so much—that I had such very bitter trials of soul together with severe bodily torments, pains, and sicknesses that I wasn't able to help myself. At other times I had more serious bodily illnesses; yet, since I didn't have the sufferings of soul, I suffered them with great gladness. But when they were all joined together the trial was so severe that it afflicted me very much. All the favors the Lord had granted me were forgotten. There only remained the memory so as to cause pain; they were like a dream. For the intellect became so stupefied that it made me walk in the midst of a thousand doubts and suspicions making it seem that I had not understood and that perhaps I had fancied the visions and that it was enough that I was deceived without my in turn deceiving good people. It seemed to me I was so evil that all the wickedness and heresies that had arisen were due to my sins (L. 30.8).

I don't mean to say that those who arrive here do not have peace; they do have it, and it is very deep. For the trials themselves are so valuable and have such good roots that although very severe they give rise to peace and happiness. From the very unhappiness caused by worldly things arises the ever so painful desire to leave this world. Any relief the soul has comes from the thought that God wants it to be living in this exile; yet even this is not enough, because in spite of all these benefits it is not entirely surrendered to God's will, as will be seen further on — although it doesn't fail to conform itself. But it conforms with a great feeling that it can do no more because no more has been given it, and with many tears. Every time it is in prayer this regret is its pain. In some ways perhaps the sorrow proceeds from the deep pain it feels at seeing that God is offended and little esteemed in this world and that many souls are lost; although those that grieve it most are Christians. Even though it sees that God's mercy is great—for, however wicked their lives, these Christians can make amends and be saved—it fears that many are being condemned (IC. V.2.10).

Chapter 13

The Church in Heaven

Christian existence means being with Christ, and for Teresa this means being where he is, "at the right hand of the Father." In terms of her head and goal, then, the Church is a heavenly Church. But since the Church is an earthly Church, she is a pilgrim Church, the pilgrim people of God whose goal is the heavenly Jerusalem. It is only when we contemplate the Church in her earthly-heavenly transitional existence that we have the whole Church in view. This heavenly Church was very much a part of Teresa's experience.

Hence, there is also another way in which God teaches the soul and speaks to it, different from the manner of speaking described previously. It is a language that belongs so to heaven that here on earth it is poorly understood, no matter how much we may desire to tell about it, if the Lord does not teach us through experience. The Lord puts what he wants the soul to know very deeply within it, and there he makes this known without image or explicit words, but in the manner of this vision we mentioned. And this manner in which God gives the soul understanding of his desires and great truths and mysteries is worthy of close attention (L. 26.6).

Returning then to the discussion of this kind of understanding, it seems to me that the Lord in every way wants this soul to have some knowledge of what goes on in heaven. I think that just as in heaven you understand without speaking (which I certainly never knew until the Lord in his goodness desired that I should see and showed himself to me in a rapture), so it is in this vision. For God and the soul understand each other only through the desire His Majesty has that it understand him, without the use of any other means devised to manifest the love these two friends have for each other. It's like the experience of two persons here on earth who love each other deeply and understand each other well; even without signs, just by a glance, it seems, they understand each other. This must be similar to what happens in the vision; without our knowing how, these two lovers gaze directly at each other, as the bridegroom says to the bride in the Song of Songs—I think I heard that it is there [Sg. 4:9;6:5] (L. 27.10).

You will ask how if nothing is seen one knows that it is Christ, or a saint, or his most glorious Mother. This, the soul will not know how to explain, nor can it understand how it knows, but it does know with the greatest certitude. It seems easier for the soul to know when the Lord speaks; but what is more amazing is that it knows the saint, who doesn't speak but seemingly is placed there by the Lord as a help to it and as its companion. Thus there are other spiritual things that one doesn't know how to explain, but through them one knows how lowly our nature is when there is question of understanding the sublime grandeurs of God, for we are incapable even of understanding these spiritual things. But let the one to whom His Majesty gives these favors receive them with admiration and praise for him. Thus he grants the soul particular graces through these favors. For since the favors are not granted to all, they should be highly esteemed; and one should strive to perform greater services. Hence the soul doesn't consider itself to be any greater because of this, and it thinks that it is the one who serves God the least among all who are in the world. This soul thinks that it is more obligated to him than anyone, and any fault it commits pierces to the core of its being, and very rightly so (IC. VI.8.6).

When the soul is in this suspension, the Lord likes to show it some secrets, things about heaven, and imaginative visions. It is able to tell of them afterward, for these remain so impressed on the memory that they are never forgotten. But when the visions are intellectual, the soul doesn't know how to speak of them. For there must be some visions during these moments that are so sublime that it's not fitting for those who live on this earth to have the further understanding necessary to explain them. However, when the soul is again in possession of its senses, it can say many things about these intellectual visions (IC. VI.4.5).

Well, now, to return to this quick rapture of the spirit. It is such that the spirit truly seems to go forth from the body. On the other hand, it is clear that this person is not dead; at least, he cannot say whether for some moments he was in the body or not. It seems to him that he was entirely in another region different from this in which we live, where there is shown another light so different from earth's light that if he were to spend his whole life trying to imagine that light, along with the other things, he would be unable to do so. It happens that within an instant so many things together are taught him that if he were to work for many years with his imagination and mind in order to systematize them he wouldn't be able to do so, not with even one thousandth part of one of them. This is not an intellectual but an imaginative vision, for the eyes of the soul see much better than do we with bodily eyes here on earth, and without words understanding of some things is given; I mean that if a person sees some saints, he knows them as well as if he had often spoken with them.

At other times, along with the things seen through the eyes of the soul by an intellectual vision, other things are represented, especially a multitude of angels with their Lord. And without seeing anything with the eyes of the body or the soul, through an admirable knowledge I will not be able to explain, there is represented what I'm saying and many other things not meant to be spoken of. Anyone who experiences them, and has more ability then I, will perhaps know how to explain them; although doing so seems to me very difficult indeed. Whether all this takes place in the body or not, I wouldn't know; at least I wouldn't swear that the soul is in the body or that the body is without the soul (IC. VI.5.7–8).

One night, being so ill that I wanted to excuse myself from mental prayer, I took my rosary in order to occupy myself in vocal prayer. I was recollected in the oratory. When the Lord desires, these devices are of little avail. I was doing this for only a short while when a spiritual rapture came upon me so forcefully that I had no power to resist it. It seemed to me I was brought into heaven, and the first persons I saw there were my father and mother. I saw things so marvelous—in as short a time as it takes to recite a Hail Mary—that I indeed remained outside myself; the experience seemed to me too great a favor. I say it lasted a short time, but perhaps it took a little longer; the impression is that the time was very short. I feared lest the experience be some illusion, although it didn't seem so to me. I didn't know what to do, because I was very ashamed to go to my confessor about this. I don't think the shame was from humility, but I thought he would make fun of me and say: Oh, what a Saint Paul you are, or a Saint Jerome, that you see heavenly things! And that these glorious saints experienced similar things made me more afraid. I did nothing but weep a great deal, for I didn't think there was any basis for my having such an experience. Finally, however much I disliked doing so, I went to my confessor; I never dared to remain silent about such things—however much I regretted having to speak of them—on account of the great fear I had of being deceived. Since he saw I was so anxious, he consoled me very much and said many kind things in order to free me from my troubled feelings.

As time went on, it happened—and continues to happen sometimes—that the Lord showed me greater secrets. There is no way in which the soul can see more than what is manifested, nor is this possible; so my soul never saw more than what the Lord wanted to show it each time. What he revealed was so great that the least part of it would have been sufficient to leave me marveling and very proficient in considering and judging all the things of life as little. I should like to be able to explain something about the least of what I came to know; and in thinking about how this can be done, I find that it is impossible. In just the difference between the light we see and the one represented there, although all is light, there is no comparison; next to that light the sun's brilliance seems to be something very blurred. In sum, the imagination, however keen it may be, cannot paint or sketch what this light is like, or any of the things the Lord gave me knowledge of. He bestows along with this knowledge a delight so sublime as to be indescribable, for all the senses rejoice to such a high degree and in such sweetness that the delight cannot be exaggerated—so it's better not to say any more.

Once, for more than an hour, since it doesn't seem to me that he left my side, the Lord was showing me admirable things in this way. He said to me: "See, Daughter, what those who are against me lose; don't neglect to tell them." Ah, my Lord, if Your Majesty doesn't give them light, what little benefit will what I say bring to those whose deeds blind them! Some persons to whom you have given light will profit from knowing about your grandeurs; but I don't think anyone who sees they are revealed to someone as dreadful and wretched as myself will believe me. May your name and mercy be blessed, because at least in myself I have seen a recognizable improvement. Afterward I wanted to remain in this state always and not return to everyday living, for the contempt that was left in me for everything earthly was great; these things all seemed to me like dung, and I see how basely we are occupied, those of us who are detained by earthly things.

Once, when I was with that lady I mentioned, I was ill with heart sickness; as I said my heart trouble was severe. Although it isn't now. Since she was very charitable, she gave orders that I be shown some of her jewels of gold and precious stone that were very valuable, especially one of the diamonds that was appraised highly. She thought they would make me happy. Recalling what the Lord has kept for us, I was laughing to myself and feeling pity at the sight of what people esteem. And I thought of how impossible it would be for me, even if I tried, to esteem those things if the Lord didn't remove from my memory the things he had shown me. In this way the soul has great dominion, so great that I don't know whether anyone who doesn't possess this dominion will understand it. It is the detachment proper and natural to us because it comes without labor on our part. God does it all, for His Majesty shows these truths in such a way, and they are so imprinted in the soul, that it is seen clearly we couldn't acquire them by ourselves in this way and in so short a time.

Likewise, little fear of death, which I always feared greatly, remained. Now death seems to me to be the easiest thing for anyone who serves God, for in a moment the soul finds it is freed from this prison and brought to rest. I think these raptures in which God carries away the spirit and reveals to it such excellent things are like the departure of the soul from the body, for in an instant these good things are seen all together. Let us omit any word about the pains suffered when the soul and body are torn from each other, for little attention should be paid to them. And the death of those who truly love God and have despised the things of this life must be more gentle.

These revelations also helped me very much, I think, in coming to know our true country and realizing that we are pilgrims here below; it is a wonderful thing to see what is there and know where we shall live. For if someone has to go to live permanently in another country, it is a great help to them in undergoing the struggle of the journey to have seen that it is a land where they will be very much at ease. These revelations are also a great help for reflecting on heavenly things and striving that our conversation be there; these things are done with ease. Doing them is very beneficial; merely to look toward heaven recollects the soul, for since the Lord desired to reveal something of what is there, the soul concentrates on it. It happens to me sometimes that those who I know live there are my companions and the ones in whom I find comfort; it seems to me that they are the ones who are truly alive and that those who live here on earth are so dead that not even the whole world, I think, affords me company, especially when I experience those impulses.

Everything I see with my bodily eyes seems to be a dream and a mockery. What I have already seen with the eyes of my soul is what I desire; and since it is seen as something far away, this life is a death. In sum, the favor the Lord grants to whomever he gives visions like these is extraordinary. They are a great help, especially in bearing a heavy cross; since nothing satisfies the soul, everything causes displeasure. And if the Lord didn't allow that sometimes the favor be forgotten, even though it again come to mind, I don't know how one could live. May he be blessed and praised forever and ever! May it please His Majesty, by the blood of his Son shed for me, since he has desired that I understand something of so many great blessings and in some way begin to enjoy them, that what happened to Lucifer, who through his own fault lost everything, may not happen to me. May he because of who he is not allow it, for I have no small fear sometimes; although, on the other hand, and very habitually, God's mercy makes me feel safe. Since he has freed me from so many sins, he will not want to let me out of his hands to go astray. This I beg your Reverence always to beg of him (L. 38.1–7).

Chapter 14

Evil

Three topics receiving less attention in the Teresian synthesis do provide us with some jolting insights into the darker side of human existence: sin, the devil, and hell. For Teresa the sinner is one who does evil before the very eyes of God. She experienced the true nature of sin with all its malice and in all its dimensions. But this experience about herself and other human beings was an experience about God as well, about his love to which sin is opposed, about his mercy, which he exercises in regard to sin. She beholds the tirelessly repeated attempts of God to draw the people of earth away from their sins. But although she was convinced of God's mercy and pardon of every sin of hers, with the increase of divine love her painful sense of the seriousness of each sin did not diminish but intensified.

Sin

Once, while approaching to receive Communion, I saw with my soul's eyes more clearly than with my bodily eyes two devils whose appearance was abominable. It seems to me their horns were wrapped around the poor priest's throat, and in the host that was going to be given to me I saw my Lord with the majesty I mentioned placed in the priest's hands, which were clearly seen to be his offender's; and I understood that that soul was in mortal sin. What would it be, my Lord, to see your beauty in the midst of such abominable figures? They were as though frightened and terrified in your presence, for it seems they would have very eagerly fled had you allowed them. This vision caused me such great disturbance I don't know how I was able to receive Communion, and I was left with a great fear, thinking that if the vision had been from God, His Majesty would not have permitted me to see the evil that was in that soul. The Lord himself told me to pray for him and that he had permitted it so that I might understand the power of the words of consecration and how God does not fail to be present, however evil the priest who recites them, and that I might see his great goodness since he places himself in those hands of his enemy, and all out of love for me and for everyone. I understand well how much more priests are obliged to be good than are others, how deplorable a thing it is to receive this most Blessed Sacrament unworthily, and how much the devil is lord over the soul in mortal sin. It did me a great deal of good and brought me deep understanding of what I owed God. May he be blessed forever and ever.

At another time something else happened to me that frightened me very much. I was at a place where a certain person died who for many years had lived a wicked life, from what I knew. But he had been sick for two years, and in some things it seems he had made amends. He died without confession, but nevertheless it didn't seem to me he would be condemned. While the body was being wrapped in its shroud, I saw many devils take that body; and it seemed they were playing with it and punishing it. This terrified me, for with large hooks they were dragging it from one devil to the other. Since I saw it buried with the honor and ceremonies accorded to all, I reflected on the goodness of God, how he did not want that soul to be defamed, but wanted the fact that it was his enemy to be concealed (L. 38.23–24).

Once while I was in prayer, the Lord showed me by a strange kind of intellectual vision what a soul is like in the state of grace. I saw this (through an intellectual vision) in the company of the most Blessed Trinity. From this company the soul received a power by which it had dominion over the whole earth. I was given an understanding of those words of the Song of Songs that say: *Veniat dilectus meus in hortum suum et comedat* [Let my beloved come into his garden and eat (Sg. 4:16)]. I was also shown how a soul in sin is without any power, but is like a person completely bound, tied, and blindfolded; for although wanting to see, such a person cannot, and cannot walk or hear, and remains in great darkness. Souls in this condition make me feel such compassion that any burden seems light to me if I can free one of them. I thought that by understanding this condition as I did—for it can be poorly explained—it wasn't possible for me to desire that anyone lose so much good or remain in so much evil (ST. 20).

True, sometimes there is greater affliction than at other times; and the affliction is also of a different kind, for the soul doesn't think about the suffering it will undergo on account of its sins but of how ungrateful it has been to One to whom it owes so much and who deserves so much to be served. For in these grandeurs God communicates to it, it understands much more about him. It is astonished at how bold it was; it weeps over its lack of respect; it thinks its foolishness was so excessive that it never finishes grieving over that foolishness when it recalls that for such base things it abandoned so great a majesty. Much more does it recall this foolishness than it does the favors it receives, though these favors are as remarkable as the one mentioned or as those still to be spoken of. These favors are like the waves of a large river in that they come and go; but the memory these souls have of their sins clings like thick mire. It always seems that these sins are alive in the memory, and this is a heavy cross.

I know a person who, apart from wanting to die in order to see God, wanted to die so as not to feel the continual pain of how ungrateful she had been to One to whom she ever owed so much and would owe. Thus it didn't seem to her that anyone's wickedness could equal her own, for she understood that there could be no one else from whom God would have had so much to put up with and to whom he had granted so many favors. As for the fear of hell, such persons don't have any. That they might lose God, at times—though seldom—distresses them very much. All their fear is that God might allow them out of his hand to offend him, and they find themselves in as miserable a state as they were once before. In regard to their own suffering or glory, they don't care. If they don't want to stay long in purgatory, the reason comes from the fact of their not wanting to be away from God—as are those who are in purgatory—rather than from the sufferings undergone there.

I wouldn't consider it safe for a soul, however favored by God, to forget that at one time it saw itself in a miserable state. Although recalling this misery is a painful thing, doing so is helpful for many. Perhaps it is because I have been so wretched that I have this opinion and am always mindful of my misery. Those who have been good will not have to feel this pain, although there will always be failures as long as we live in this mortal body. No relief is afforded this suffering by the thought that our Lord has already pardoned and forgotten the sins. Rather, it adds to the suffering to see so much goodness and realize that favors are granted to one who deserves nothing but hell. I think such a realization was a great martyrdom for Saint Peter and the Magdalene. Since their love for God had grown so deep and they had received so many favors and come to know the grandeur and majesty of God, the remembrance of their misery would have been difficult to suffer, and they would have suffered it with tender sentiments (IC. VI.7.2–4).

But what will these souls feel on seeing that they could lack so great a blessing? Seeing this makes them proceed more carefully and seek to draw strength from their weakness so as not to abandon through their own fault any opportunity to please God more. The more favored they are by His Majesty the more they are afraid and fearful of themselves. And since through his grandeurs they have come to a greater knowledge of their own miseries, and their sins become more serious to them, they often go about like the publican not daring to raise their eyes. At other times they go about desiring to die so as to be safe; although, with the love they have, soon they again want to live in order to serve him, as we said. And in everything concerning themselves they trust in his mercy. Sometimes the many favors make them feel more annihilated, for they fear that just as a ship too heavily laden sinks to the bottom they will go down too (IC. VII.3.14).

The Devil

> The devil is the foe of God and the enemy of human beings, a tempter endeavoring to deceive, lead them into sin, and obstruct God's plan. His presence causes disquiet, restlessness, and affliction. But he is afraid of God or anyone who draws close to God. He wants attention, so if we pay no attention to him he will go elsewhere.

When the words are from the devil, not only do they fail to have good effects but they leave bad ones. This happened to me no more than two or three times, and I was then advised by the Lord that the words were from the devil. Besides the great dryness that remains, there is a disquiet in the soul like that which the Lord permitted many other times when my soul suffered severe temptations and trials of different kinds. Although this disquiet often torments me as I shall say further on, one is unable to understand where the disquiet comes from. It seems the soul resists; it is agitated and afflicted without knowing why because what he says is not evil but good. I wonder if one spirit doesn't feel the presence of the other spirit. The consolation and delight that he gives is, in my opinion, very markedly different. He could deceive with these consolations someone who does not have or has not had other consolations from God (L. 25.10).

There was no doubt, in my opinion, that they were afraid of me, for I remained so calm and so unafraid of them all. All the fears I usually felt left me—even to this day. For although I sometimes saw them, as I shall relate afterward, I no longer had hardly any fear of them; rather it seemed they were afraid of me.

I was left with a mastery over them truly given by the Lord of all; I pay no more attention to them than to flies. I think they're cowards that when they observe they are esteemed but little, their strength leaves them. These enemies don't know how to attack head-on, save those whom they see surrender to them, or when God permits them to do so for the greater good of his servants whom they tempt and torment. May it please His Majesty that we fear him whom we ought to fear and understand that more harm can come to us from one venial sin than from all hell together—for this is so (L. 25.20).

I said that this union was not some kind of dreamy state, because even if the experience in the dwelling place that was just mentioned is abundant the soul remains doubtful that it was union. It doubts whether it imagined the experience; whether it was asleep; whether the experience was given by God; or whether the devil transformed himself into an angel of light. It is left with a thousand suspicions. That it has them is good, for, as I have said, even our own nature can sometimes deceive us in that dwelling place. Though there is not so much room for poisonous things to enter, some tiny lizards do enter; since these lizards have slender heads they can poke their heads in anywhere. And even though they do no harm, especially if one pays no attention to them, as I said, they are often a bother since they are little thoughts proceeding from the imagination and from what I mentioned. But however slender they may be, these little lizards cannot enter this fifth dwelling place; for there is neither imagination, nor memory, nor intellect that can impede this good. And I would dare say that if the prayer is truly that of union with God the devil cannot even enter or do any damage. His Majesty is so joined and united with the essence of the soul that the devil will not approach nor will he even know about this secret. And this is obvious. Since as they say, he doesn't know our mind, he will have less knowledge of something so secret; for God doesn't even entrust this to our own mind. Oh what a great good, a state in which this accursed one does us no harm! Thus the soul is left with such wonderful blessings because God works within it without anyone disturbing him, not even ourselves. What will he not give, who is so fond of giving and who can give all that he wants? (IC. V.1.5).

You may wonder why greater security is present in this favor than in other things. In my opinion, these are the reasons: First, the devil never gives delightful pain like this. He can give the savor and delight that seem to be spiritual, but he doesn't have the power to join pain—and so much of it—to the spiritual quiet and delight of the soul. For all of his powers are on the outside, and the pains he causes are never, in my opinion, delightful or peaceful, but disturbing and contentious. Second, this delightful tempest comes from a region other than those regions of which he can be lord. Third, the favor brings wonderful benefits to the soul, the more customary of which are the determination to suffer for God, the desire to have many trials, and the determination to withdraw from earthly satisfactions and conversations and other similar things (IC. VI.2.6).

Hell

Teresa's frightful description of her vision of hell has become classic. The vision was an intensely painful one and at the same time most fruitful. Six years later she could still feel and relive its terrifying effects. It was not just a passing vision or the only one. But what is noteworthy in her vision of hell is not the horror of it but her realization that the Lord in his mercy freed her from that place reserved for her.

A long time after the Lord had already granted me many of the favors I've mentioned and other very lofty ones, while I was in prayer one day, I suddenly found that, without knowing how, I had seemingly been put in hell. I understood that the Lord wanted me to see the place the devils had prepared there for me and which I merited because of my sins. This experience took place within the shortest space of time, but even were I to live for many years I think it would be impossible for me to forget it. The entrance it seems to me was similar to a very long and narrow alleyway, like an oven, low and dark and confined; the floor seemed to me to consist of dirty, muddy water emitting a foul stench and swarming with putrid vermin. At the end of the alleyway a hole that looked like a small cupboard was hollowed out in the wall; there I found I was placed in a cramped condition. All of this was delightful to see in comparison with what I felt there. What I have described can hardly be exaggerated.

What I felt, it seems to me, cannot even begin to be exaggerated; nor can it be understood. I experienced a fire in the soul that I don't know how I could describe. The bodily pains were so unbearable that though I had suffered excruciating ones in this life and according to what doctors say, the worst that can be suffered on earth (for all my nerves were shrunken when I was paralyzed, plus many other sufferings of many kinds that I endured, and even some, as I said, caused by the devil), these were all nothing in comparison with the ones I experienced there. I saw furthermore that they would go on without end and without ever ceasing. This, however, was nothing next to the soul's agonizing: a constriction, a suffocation, an affliction so keenly felt and with such a despairing and tormenting unhappiness that I don't know how to word it strongly enough. To say the experience is as though the soul were continually being wrested from the body would be insufficient, for it would make you think somebody else is taking away the life, whereas here it is the soul itself that tears itself in pieces. The fact is that I don't know how to give a sufficiently powerful description of that interior fire and that despair, coming in addition to such extreme torments and pains. I didn't see who inflicted them on me, but, as it seemed to me, I felt myself burning and crumbling; and I repeat the worst was that interior fire and despair.

Being in such a unwholesome place, so unable to hope for any consolation, I found it impossible either to sit down or to lie down, nor was there any room, even though they put me in this kind of hole made in the wall. Those walls, which were terrifying to see, closed in on themselves and suffocated everything. There was no light, but all was enveloped in the blackest darkness. I don't understand how this could be, that everything painful to see was visible.

The Lord didn't want me to see any more of hell at that time. Afterward I saw another vision of frightful things, the punishment of some vices. With respect to the sight they seemed much more frightening, but since I didn't feel the pain, they didn't cause me so much fear. For in the former vision the Lord wanted me actually to feel those spiritual torments and afflictions, as though the body were suffering. I don't know how such an experience was possible, but I well understood that it was a great favor and that the Lord desired me to see with my own eyes the place his mercy had freed me from. It amounts to nothing to hear these pains spoken of, nor have I at other times thought about different torments (although not many, since my soul did not fare well with such fearful thoughts; that is, that devils tear off the flesh with pincers, or other various tortures I've read about) that are anything in comparison to this pain; it is something different. In sum, as a resemblance to the reality, being burned here on earth is very little when compared to being burned by the fire that is there.

I was left terrified, and still am now in writing about this almost six years later, and it seems to me that on account of the fear my natural heat fails me right here and now. Thus I recall no time of trial or suffering in which it doesn't seem to me that everything that can be suffered here on earth is nothing; so I think in a way we complain without reason. Hence I repeat that this experience was one of the greatest favors the Lord granted me because it helped me very much to lose fear of the tribulations and contradictions of this life as well as to grow strong enough to suffer them and give thanks to the Lord who freed me, as it now appears to me, from such everlasting and terrible evils.

Since that time, as I say, everything seems to me easy when compared to undergoing for a moment what I suffered there in hell. I marvel how after having often read books in which the pains of hell were somewhat explained I didn't fear them or take them for what they were. Where was I? How could I find relaxation in anything when I was causing myself to go to such an evil place? May you be blessed, my God, forever! How obvious it is that you loved me much more than I did myself! How many times, my Lord, have you freed me from so dark a prison, and how often have I put myself in it again against your will (L. 32.3–5)!

Chapter 15

Grace

As already noted, Jesus Christ showed himself to Teresa as the source of our capacity to appear before God, as the gate and channel for every grace. In speaking of grace as the gift of God, who gives us his Son, she has in mind both the source of the gift in the One who gives and the effect of the gift in the one who receives. In a keen awareness of her own unworthiness, Teresa finds that grace superabounds because of God's sovereign generosity.

An Undeserved Gift

God is very pleased to see a soul that humbly takes his Son as mediator and that loves this Son so much that even when His Majesty desires to raise it to very lofty contemplation, as I have said, it is aware of its unworthiness, saying with Saint Peter: "Depart from me, Lord, for I am a sinful man" [Lk. 10:4].

Such has been my experience; it's the way God has led my soul. Others will journey, as I've said, by another short cut. What I have come to understand is that this whole groundwork of prayer is based on humility and that the more a soul lowers itself in prayer the more God raises it up. I don't recall his ever having granted me one of the very notable favors of which I shall speak later if not at a time when I was brought to nothing at the sight of my wretchedness. And so as to help me know myself, His Majesty even strove to give me an understanding of things that I wouldn't have known how to imagine. I hold that when the soul does something on its own to help itself in this prayer of union, even though this may at first seem beneficial, it will very soon fall again since it doesn't have a good foundation. I fear that it will never attain true poverty of spirit, which means being at rest in labors and dryness and not seeking consolation or comfort in prayer—for earthly consolation has already been abandoned—but seeking consolation in trials for love of him who always lived in the midst of them. Although if some consolation is felt, it shouldn't cause the disturbance and pain it does to some persons who think that if they aren't always working with the intellect and striving for devotion all is lost—as though so great a blessing could be merited by their labor. I don't say that they shouldn't strive carefully to remain in God's presence, but that if they can't even get a good thought, as I've mentioned elsewhere, they shouldn't kill themselves. We are useless servants, what do we think we can do? (L. 22.11).

Grace and the Sacraments

Even a soul that has reached the mystical union of the fourth water may feel the misfortune of falling into sin. And then it is the power of the sacraments that bring her comfort and heal her wounds. What Teresa particularly experienced in the sacraments, especially the Eucharist, was the Lord's presence, always a healing and strengthening presence. She beheld there the fulfillment of his promise to remain with us until the end of time. Since his ascension, Jesus' bodily presence has passed into the sacraments. In giving us his real presence, Jesus has handed over to us his life and his being, the whole of his humanity and divinity, all the moments and events of his life and his relationship with his Father. His presence in the sacraments is a living, breathing, acting presence, not a static thing.

O my Jesus! What a sight it is when you through your mercy return to offer your hand and raise up a soul that has fallen in sin after having reached this stage! How such a soul knows the multitude of your grandeurs and mercies and its own misery! In this state it is in truth consumed and knows your splendors. Here it doesn't dare raise its eyes, and here it raises them up so as to know what it owes you. Here it becomes a devotee of the queen of heaven so that she might appease you; here it invokes the help of the saints that fell after having been called by you. Here it seems that everything you give it is undeserved because it sees that it doesn't merit the ground on which it treads. Here, in approaching the sacraments, it has the living faith to see the power that God has placed in them; it praises you because you have left such a medicine and ointment for our wounds and because this medicine not only covers these wounds but takes them away completely. It is amazed by all this. And who, Lord of my soul, wouldn't be amazed by so much mercy and a favor so large for a betrayal so ugly and abominable? I don't know why my heart doesn't break as I write this! For I am a wretched person! (L. 19.5).

Ask the Father, daughters, together with the Lord, to give you your Spouse "this day" so that you will not be seen in this world without him. To temper such great happiness it's sufficient that he remain disguised in these accidents of bread and wine. This is torment enough for anyone who has no other love than him nor any other consolation. Beg him not to fail you, and to give you the dispositions to receive him worthily (W. 34.3).

As for ourselves, let us ask the Eternal Father that we might merit to receive our heavenly bread in such a way that the Lord may reveal himself to the eyes of our soul and make himself thereby known since our bodily eyes cannot delight in beholding him, because he is so hidden. Such knowledge is another kind of satisfying and delightful sustenance that maintains life (W. 34.5).

Do you think this heavenly food fails to provide sustenance, even for these bodies, that it is not a great medicine even for bodily ills? I know that it is. I know a person with serious illnesses, who often experiences great pain, who through this bread had them taken away as though by a gesture of the hand and was made completely well. This is a common experience, and the illnesses are very recognizable, for I don't think they could be feigned. And because the wonders this most sacred bread effects in those who worthily receive it are well known, I will not mention many that could be mentioned regarding this person I've spoken of. I was able to know of them, and I know that this is no lie. But the Lord had given her such living faith that when she heard some persons saying they would have liked to have lived at the time Christ our Good walked in the world, she used to laugh to herself. She wondered what more they wanted since in the most Blessed Sacrament they had him just as truly present as he was then.

But I know that for many years, when she received Communion, this person, though she was not very perfect, strove to strengthen her faith so that in receiving her Lord it was as if, with her bodily eyes, she saw him enter her house. Since she believed that this Lord truly entered her poor home, she freed herself from all exterior things when it was possible and entered to be with him. She strove to recollect the senses so that all of them would take notice of so great a good, I mean that they would not impede the soul from recognizing it. She considered she was at his feet and wept with the Magdalene, no more nor less than if she were seeing him with her bodily eyes in the house of the Pharisee. And even though she didn't feel devotion, faith told her that he was indeed there.

. . . Now, then, if when he went about in the world the mere touch of his robes cured the sick, why doubt, if we have faith, that miracles will be worked while he is within us and that he will give what we ask of him, since he is in our house? His Majesty is not accustomed to paying poorly for his lodging if the hospitality is good (W. 34.6–8).

The Waters of Grace

> In her contemplative experiences of the beauty of a soul in grace,
> Teresa, as noted, perceived directly the contrast between a just
> soul and a soul in sin. She observed a clear distinction between
> the fundamental dignity of the soul as an image of God and as one
> endowed with a new grace-filled beauty, a beauty which attracts
> both God and other human beings. Through its communion with
> God, made possible through Jesus Christ, the soul in prayer
> drinks from the torrents of God's delights, and becomes in its life
> and actions gradually more God-like.

This water of great blessings and favors that the Lord gives
here makes the virtues grow incomparably better than in the
previous degree of prayer, for the soul is now ascending above its
misery and receiving a little knowledge of the delights of glory.
This water I believe makes the virtues grow better and also brings
the soul much closer to the true Virtue, which is God, from
whence come all the virtues. His Majesty is beginning to communicate himself to this soul, and he wants it to experience how he
is doing so.

In arriving here it begins soon to lose its craving for earthly
things—and little wonder! It sees clearly that one moment of the
enjoyment of glory cannot be experienced here below, neither
are there riches, or sovereignties, or honors, or delights that are
able to provide a brief moment of that happiness, for it is a true
happiness that, it is seen, satisfies us. In earthly things it would
seem to me a marvel were we ever to understand just where we
can find this satisfaction, for there is never lacking in these
earthly things both the "yes" and the "no." During the time of
this prayer, everything is "yes." The "no" comes afterward upon
seeing that the delight is ended and that one cannot recover
it—nor does one know how. Were one to crush self with
penances and prayer and all the rest, it would profit little if the
Lord did not desire to give this delight. God in his greatness
desires that this soul understand that he is so close it no longer
needs to send him messengers but can speak with him itself and

not by shouting since he is so near that when it merely moves its lips, he understands it.

It seems impertinent to say this since we know that God always understands us and is with us. There is no doubt about this understanding and presence. But our Emperor and Lord desires that in this prayer we know that he understands us, and what his presence does, and that he wants to begin to work in the soul in a special way. All of this that the Lord desires is manifest in the great interior and exterior satisfaction he gives the soul and in the difference there is, as I said, between this delight and happiness and the delights of earth, for this delight seems to fill the void that through our sins we have caused in the soul. This satisfaction takes place in its very intimate depths, and the soul doesn't know where the satisfaction comes from or how, nor frequently does it know what to do or what to desire or what to ask for. It seems it has found everything at once and doesn't know what it has found.

Nor do I know how to explain this experience because for so many things learning is necessary. Here it would be helpful to explain well the difference between a general and a particular grace—for there are many who are ignorant of this difference—and how the Lord desires that the soul in this prayer almost see with its own eyes, as they say, this particular grace. Learning is also required to explain many other things, which I perhaps did not express correctly. But since what I say is going to be checked by persons who will recognize any error, I'm not worrying about it. In matters of theology as well as in those of the spirit I know that I can be mistaken; yet, since this account will end in good hands, these learned men will understand and remove what is erroneous (L. 14.5–6).

Thus it lives a laborious life and always with the cross, but it continues to grow rapidly. When it is observed by its companions it seems to be at the summit. Within a short while it is much improved because God always goes on favoring it more. It is his soul; it is he who has taken it into his charge, and thus he illumines it. For it seems that by his assistance, he is ever guarding it from offending him and favoring it and awakening it to his service.

When my soul reached this stage where God granted it such a great favor, the evil in me disappeared, and the Lord gave me strength to break away from it. It didn't bother me to be amid the occasions of falling and with people who formerly distracted me any more than if there were no occasions at all; what used to do me harm was helping me. All things were a means for my knowing and loving God more, for seeing what I owed him, and for regretting what I had been (L. 21.10).

It seems I have left you confused by saying "if it is union" and that there are other unions. And indeed how true it is that there are! Even though these unions regard vain things, the devil will use such things to transport us when they are greatly loved. But he doesn't do so in the way God does, or with the delight and satisfaction of soul, or with the peace and joy. This union is above all earthly joys, above all delights, above all consolations, and still more than that. It doesn't matter where those spiritual or earthly joys come from, for the feeling is very different as you will have experienced. I once said that the difference is like that between feeling something on the rough outer covering of the body or in the marrow of the bones. And that was right on the mark (IC. V.1.6).

Chapter 16

The Works and Merits of the Wayfarer

Teresa perceives clearly the merits of Christ communicated to her soul as a personal endowment given by her Lord. Behind her works she notes the unique work of God: God's own Son. Her good works are thus experienced as the overflow of the divine work, although they also demand a personal effort, on her part, an engagement, a choice.

Once while I was experiencing great distress over having offended God, he said to me: "All your sins are before me as though they were not; in the future make every effort, for your trials are not over" (ST 46).

Perhaps he will respond as he did to a person who before a crucifix was reflecting with deep affliction that she had never had anything to give to God, or anything to give up for him. The Crucified, himself, in consoling her told her he had given her all the sufferings and trials he had undergone in his Passion so that she could have them as her own to offer his Father. The comfort and enrichment was such that, according to what I have heard from her, she cannot forget the experience. Rather, every time she sees how miserable she is, she gets encouragement and consolation from remembering those words.

I could mention here some other experiences like this, for since I have dealt with so many holy and prayerful persons, I know about many such experiences; but I want to limit myself lest you think I am speaking of myself. What I said seems to me very beneficial to help you understand how pleased our Lord is that we know ourselves and strive to reflect again and again on our poverty and misery and on how we possess nothing that we have not received. So, my sisters, courage is necessary for this knowledge and for the many other graces given to the soul the Lord has brought to this stage. And when there is humility, courage, in my opinion, is even more necessary for this knowledge of one's own misery. May the Lord give us this humility because of who he is (IC. VI.5.6).

Someone could think that if turning back is so bad it would be better never to begin but to remain outside the castle. I have already told you at the beginning—and the Lord himself tells you—that anyone who walks in danger perishes in it and that the door of entry to this castle is prayer. Well now, it is foolish to think that we will enter heaven without entering into ourselves, coming to know ourselves, reflecting on our misery and what we owe God, and begging him often for mercy. The Lord himself says: No one will ascend to my Father but through me [Jn. 14:6] (I don't know if he says it this way—I think he does) and whoever sees me sees my Father [Jn. 14:9]. Well, if we never look at him or reflect on what we owe him and the death he suffered for us, I don't know how we'll be able to know him or do works in his service. And what value can faith have without works and without joining them to the merits of Jesus Christ, our Good? Or who will awaken us to love this Lord?

May it please His Majesty to give us understanding of how much we cost him, of how the servant is no greater than his master, and that we must work in order to enjoy his glory. And we need to pray for this understanding so that we aren't always entering into temptation (IC. II.1.11).

Well, I say that it is dangerous to count the number of years in which you have practiced prayer; even though humility may be present, I think there can remain a kind of feeling that you deserve something for the service. I don't mean that you don't gain merit and that you will not be well paid. But I consider it certain that spiritual persons who think that they deserve these delights of spirit for the many years they have practiced prayer will not ascend to the summit of the spiritual life. Isn't it enough that God take them by the hand to keep them from committing the offenses they did before they practiced prayer, without their wanting, so to speak, to sue God for money? I don't think it shows profound humility. Indeed, it could; but I consider it audacity. I don't think that I, who have little humility, would ever have dared to do so. Now it might be that since I have never served, I have never asked; perhaps if I had served, I would desire more than anyone that the Lord repay me.

I don't say that a soul will not grow or that God will not give this increase if its prayer has been humble, but I say that those years of service should be forgotten; for in comparison with one drop of the blood the Lord shed for us, everything we do is disgusting. And if in serving more we become more indebted, what is this we seek? For if we pay one *maravedi* of the debt, we are given a thousand *ducats* in return. Let us out of love for God set aside these judgments because they belong to him. These comparisons are always bad, even in earthly matters; what must they amount to in matters that only God knows about? And His Majesty showed it well when he paid as much to the workers who came last as to those who came first (L. 39.15–16).

Well see here, daughters, what we can do through the help of God: His Majesty himself, as he does in this prayer of union, becomes the dwelling place we build for ourselves. It seems I'm saying that we can build up God and take him away since I say that he is the dwelling place and we ourselves can build it so as to place ourselves in it. And, indeed, we can! Not that we can take God away or build him up, but we can take away from ourselves and build up, as do these little silkworms. For we will not have finished doing all that we can in this work when, to the little we do, which is nothing, God will unite himself, with his greatness, and give it such high value that the Lord himself will become the reward of this work. Thus, since it was he who paid the highest price, His Majesty wants to join our little labors with the great ones he suffered so that all the work may become one (IC. V.2.5).

Once while desiring to render some service to our Lord, I was thinking about how little I was able to do for him and I said to myself: "Why, Lord, do you desire my works?" He answered: "In order to see your will, daughter"(ST. 47).

The Merits of the Wayfarer

> Approaching the end of her life, Teresa gives a veiled reference to a clear mystical perception of the merits accumulated by her wayfaring soul. But they are all the work of the mercy of God. And so her only trust is in his mercy, and her one desire is to serve God and live for his honor and glory.

But what will these souls feel on seeing that they could lack so great a blessing? Seeing this makes them proceed more carefully and seek to draw strength from their weakness so as not to abandon through their own fault any opportunity to please God more. The more favored they are by His Majesty the more they are afraid and fearful of themselves. And since through his grandeurs they have come to a greater knowledge of their own miseries, and their sins become more serious to them, they often go about like the publican not daring to raise their eyes. At other times they go about desiring to die so as to be safe; although, with the love they have, soon they again want to live in order to serve him, as we said. And in everything concerning themselves they trust in his mercy. Sometimes the many favors make them feel more annihilated, for they fear that just as a ship too heavily laden sinks to the bottom they will go down too (IC. VII.3.14).

Oh, who would be able to explain to Your Excellency the quiet and calm my soul experiences! It is so certain it will enjoy God that it thinks it already enjoys the possession of him, although not the fruition. It's as though one had given another, with heavily warranted deeds, the promise of a large revenue that that other will be able to enjoy at a certain time. But until then, this latter person enjoys only the promise that she shall have the fruition of this revenue. Despite the gratitude the soul feels, it would rather not rejoice. For it thinks it hasn't deserved anything other than to serve, even if this service be through much suffering. And sometimes it even seems to it that the period from now until the end of the world would be a short time to serve the one who gave it this possession. Because, to put it truthfully, this soul is no longer in part subject to the miseries of the world as it used to be. For although it suffers more, this is only on the surface. The soul is like a lord in his castle, and so it doesn't lose its peace; although this security doesn't remove a great fear of offending God and of not getting rid of all that would be a hindrance to serving him. The soul rather proceeds more cautiously, but it goes about so forgetful of self that it thinks it has partly lost its being. In this state everything is directed to the honor of God, to the greater fulfillment of his will, and to his glory (ST. 65).

Chronology

1515   On 28 March Teresa is born in Avila and baptized on 4 April.

1522   After learning about her Christian faith and how to read she becomes fascinated with the lives of the saints and convinces her brother Rodrigo to run away from home with her to become a martyr in the land of the Moors, but they do not get far and are brought home.

1526   She becomes captivated by books of chivalry and even tries writing one herself, which has been lost.

1528   Her mother dies. Teresa goes to the shrine of *La Virgen de la Caridad* to ask Mary to take on the role of mother to her.

1531   Worried about some of the friendships she begins to develop, her father places her in a convent school directed by Augustinian nuns.

1535   After much hesitation she comes to a definite decision about being a nun and on 2 November enters the Carmelite Monastery of the Incarnation.

1536   On 2 November she receives the Carmelite habit, beginning her novitiate year.

1537   On 3 November she makes profession.

1538   Teresa becomes seriously ill and leaves the monastery to seek a cure in Becedas. She stays some time with her uncle Don Pedro in Hortigosa who gives her a book by Francisco de Osuna, *The Third Spiritual Alphabet*. In this book she learns about the prayer of recollection and begins to practice it.

1539   In July she is brought back to Avila gravely ill and remains a paralytic for three years.

1542   Teresa feels cured through the intercession of St. Joseph.

1543   Teresa cares for her sick father, who dies on 26 December.

1544   She returns to her practice of prayer with the encouragement of her father's spiritual director, Vicente Barrón, O.P.

1554   After years of struggle in her spiritual life, she experiences during Lent a conversion before an image of the wounded Christ. Her mystical life begins. She turns to the Jesuit fathers in Avila for spiritual direction.

1556   She receives the grace of spiritual betrothal. Some priests begin to frighten her by attributing her favors from God to the devil.

1559   On 29 June, Teresa receives her first intellectual vision of Christ.

1560   On 25 January, she receives a vision of the risen Christ and later receives the grace of the transpiercing of the soul. St. Peter of Alcanatara assures Teresa that her experiences are God's work. She has a terrifying vision of hell, which leads to her desire to found a small community of nuns who would live according to the primitive rule of Carmel like the early hermits on Mount Carmel.

1561   Teresa receives orders from her provincial to go to Toledo to serve as a companion to the wealthy Doña Luisa de la Cerda who had recently lost her husband.

1562   With the help of St. Peter of Alcantara and the bishop of Avila, Don Alvaro de Mendoza, Teresa receives permission to found her new monastery in Avila, which took place on 24 August and was dedicated to St. Joseph. They eventually were referred to as discalced Carmelites because as a symbol of their return to the primitive rule they wore hemp sandals rather than shoes.

1565   Concludes the final redaction of *The Book of Her Life*.

1566   The year in which she probably composed her two redactions of *The Way of Perfection*, which explains the spirituality behind her nuns' way of observing the primitive rule.

1567   The general of the Carmelites, Giovanni Battista Rossi, visits Avila and urges Teresa to found more monasteries like St. Joseph's. On 15 August, Teresa founds a new monastery in Medina del Campo. On 16 August she receives permission to found similar monasteries for friars. She later speaks with St. John of the Cross and encourages him to join her in her plan for the friars.

1568   On 11 April she makes a foundation in Malagón, the home town of Doña Luisa de la Cerda. On 15 August she makes a foundation in Valladolid. John of the Cross accompanies her and learns about the Teresian way of life. On 28 November a few friars begin living in this new Teresian way in Duruelo.

1569   On 14 May she makes a foundation in Toledo and on 23 June, another one in Pastrana. On 26 August, Pedro Fernández, O.P., and Francisco Vargas, O.P., are appointed the apostolic visitators for Castile and Andalusia respectively. This marks the beginning of troubles since Rossi had not given permission for foundations in Andalusia.

1570   On 1 November Teresa makes a foundation in Salamanca.

1571   On 25 January, assisted by John of the Cross, she makes a foundation in Alba de Tormes. On 14 October, appointed by the visitator, she becomes the prioress at the Incarnation.

1572   Teresa arranges to have John of the Cross come as confessor and chaplain. On 18 November she receives the grace of spiritual marriage.

1573   The discalced friars begin making foundations in Andalusia. On 25 August Teresa begins writing *The Book of Her Foundations*.

1574   On 19 March, accompanied by John of the Cross, she makes a foundation in Segovia. She writes her *Meditations on the Song of Songs*.

1575   On 24 February Teresa makes a foundation in Beas, not knowing that it was in the ecclesiastical province of Andalusia. There she meets Father Gracián, a son of one of the king's secretaries, who had joined the discalced friars and been given authority by the nuncio, Ormaneto, over the discalced friars and nuns. He orders Teresa to make a foundation in Seville, which she does on 29 May. She receives a command from the order to stop making foundations and return to Castile, for the order's chapter at Piacenza (Italy) had decided to rein in the discalced movement. On 28 May she sets out on her journey back to Castile in the company of her brother Lorenzo recently returned from America. She takes up her residence temporarily in Toledo on 23 June.

1577   On 2 June, under orders from Gracián, she begins writing *The Interior Castle*. On 18 June, the nuncio, Ormaneto, who had been favorable to the discalced cause, dies. In July Teresa returns to Avila. On 29 November she concludes *The Interior Castle*. On 3 December John of the Cross is unjustly imprisoned on account of the confusion arising from the chapter in Piacenza. On 24 December, falling down the stairs, Teresa breaks her left arm, which was never reset properly.

1578   On 23 July the new nuncio, Sega, takes away Gracián's powers. He metes out punishment to some of the leaders among the discalced friars.

1579   On 1 April Sega names Teresa's former provincial, Angel de Salazar, vicar general for the discalced friars and nuns. This brings about a modicum of peace for the discalced Carmelites.

1580   On 28 January, Salazar gives Teresa permission to make a foundation in Villanueva de la Jara, which she does on 25 February. On 5 May, Gracián receives once more his faculties as provincial of the discalced friars and nuns. On 22 June through a papal brief *Pia consideratione* the discalced Carmelites are allowed to form a separate province. On 29 December Teresa makes a foundation in Palencia.

1581   On 3 June she makes a foundation in Soria. On 10 September she is elected prioress of St. Joseph's in Avila.

1582   On 2 January accompanied by Gracián, Teresa leaves for a foundation in Burgos, a most difficult journey because of her poor health and the bad winter weather. Not until 19 April is she able to overcome all opposition in Burgos and make the foundation. On her return to Avila in September she is given orders by her provincial to go to Alba de Tormes because of a request by the Duchess of Alba. Arriving exhausted in Alba on 20 September, her health continues to deteriorate, and on 29 September she goes to bed seriously ill never to get up again. On 4 October at 9 P.M., at the age of sixty-seven, Teresa dies. Because of the Gregorian reform of the calendar that year, the day became 15 October.

1614   On 24 April Teresa is beatified by Paul V.

1622   On 12 March she is canonized by Gregory XV along with Saints Isidore, Ignatius Loyola, Francis Xavier, and Philip Neri.

1970   On 27 September Teresa is declared a Doctor of the Church by Paul VI, and becomes the first woman saint to be so recognized.

Bibliography

Spanish Editions

Obras de Santa Teresa de Jesús. Ed. Silverio de Santa Teresa. Vols. 1-9 in *Biblioteca Mística Carmelitana*. Burgos: El Monte Carmelo, 1915-1924.

Santa Teresa: Obras Completas. Ed. Tomás Alvarez. Burgos: El Monte Carmelo, 1994.

Santa Teresa: Cartas. Ed. Tomás Alvarez. Burgos: El Monte Carmelo, 1997.

Santa Teresa de Jesús: Obras Completas. Ed. Efrén de la Madre de Dios and Otger Steggink. Madrid: La Editorial Católica, 1976.

English Editions

The Collected Works of St. Teresa of Avila. Trans. Kieran Kavanaugh and Otilio Rodriguez. 3 vols. Washington, D.C.: ICS Publications, 1976-1985.

The Collected Letters of St. Teresa of Avila. Trans. Kieran Kavanaugh. Vol 1. Washington, D.C.: ICS Publications, 2001.

The Complete Works of St. Teresa of Jesus. Tran. E. Allison Peers. 3 vols. London: Sheed and Ward, 1958.

The Letters of Saint Teresa of Jesus. Tran. E. Allison Peers. 2 vols. London: Sheed and Ward, 1980

Biographies

Alvarez, Tomás and Fernando Domingo. *Saint Teresa of Avila: A Spiritual Adventure*. Tran. Cristopher O'Mahony. Washington, D.C.: ICS Publications, 1982

Auclair, Marcel. *St. Teresa of Avila*. Tran. Kathleen Pond. New York: Pantheon Books, 1953.

Clissold, Stephen. *St. Teresa of Avila*. New York: The Seabury Press, 1982.

Efrén de la Madre de Dios and Otger Steggink. *Santa Teresa y Su Tiempo*. 3 vols. Salamanca: Universidad Pontificia de Salamanca, 1982.

Medwick, Cathleen. *Teresa of Avila: The Progress of a Soul*. New York: Alfred A. Knopf, 1999.

Papasogli, Giorgio. *St. Teresa of Avila*. Tran. Gloria Anzilotti. Jamaica Plain, MA: Society of St. Paul, 1988.

Walsh, William Thomas. *Saint Teresa of Avila*. Milwaukee: Bruce Publishing Company, 1943.

Prayers

Alvarez, Thomas, comp. *The Prayers of St. Teresa of Avila*. New York: New City Press, 1990

Griffin, Michael D. ed. *Lingering with My Lord: Post-Communion Experiences of St. Teresa of Avila*. New York: Alba House, 1985.

Studies

Barrientos, Alberto, ed. *Introducción a la lectura de Santa Teresa*. Madrid: Editorial de Espiritualidad, 1978.

Beevers, John. *St. Teresa of Avila*. New York: Doubleday, 1961

Bielecki, Tessa. *Teresa of Avila: Mystical Writings*. New York: Crossroad, 1994

Bilinkoff, Jodi. *The Avila of St. Teresa: Religious Reform in a Sixteenth-Century City*. Ithaca, NY: Cornell University Press, 1989.

_____. *Carmelite Studies: Centenary of St. Teresa*. Vol. 3, edited by John Sullivan. Washington, DC: ICS Publications, 1984.

Chorpenning, Joseph F. *The Divine Romance: Teresa of Avila's Narrative Theology*. Chicago: Loyola University Press, 1992.

D'Souza, Gregory. *Teresian Mysticism and Yoga*. Mangalore, India: Sarada Press, 1981.

Frohlich, Mary. *The Intersubjectivity of The Mystic: A Study of Teresa's Interior Castle*. Atlanta, Georgia, 1993.

Glynn, Joseph. *The Eternal Mystic: St. Teresa of Avila, The First Woman Doctor of the Church*. New York: Vantage Press, 1982.

Gross, Francis L. Jr. with Toni Perior Gross. *The Making of a Mystic: Seasons in the Life of Theresa of Avila*. Albany, NY: State University of New York Press, 1993.

Haneman, Sr. Mary Alphonsetta. *The Spirituality of St. Teresa of Avila*. Boston: St. Paul Editions, 1983.

Hoornaert, Rodolphe. *Saint Teresa in Her Writings*. New York: Benziger Brothers, 1931.

Luti, Mary J. *Teresa of Avila's Way*. Collegeville, MN: The Liturgical Press, 1991.

Petersson, Robert T. *The Art of Ecstasy Teresa, Bernini, and Crashaw*. New York: Atheneum, 1970.

Ramge, Sebastian. *An Introduction to the Writings of St. Teresa*. Chicago: Henry Regnery Company, 1963.

Slade, Carole. *St. Teresa of Avila: Author of a Heroic Life*. Berkely: University of California Press, 1995.

Thomas, Fr. and Gabriel, Fr. *St. Teresa of Avila: Studies in Her Life, Doctrine and Times*. Westminster, MD: The Newman Press, 1963.

Weber, Alison. *Teresa of Avila and the Rhetoric of Femininity*. Princeton: Princeton University Press, 1990.

Welch, John. *Spiritual Pilgrims: Carl Jung and Teresa of Avila*. New York: Paulist Press, 1982.

Williams, Rowan. *Teresa of Avila*. Harrisburg, PA: Morehouse, 1991.

ALSO AVAILABLE IN THE SAME SERIES FROM NEW CITY PRESS

JOHN OF THE CROSS—THE ASCENT TO JOY
MARC FOLEY, O.C.D. (ed.)
ISBN 1-56548-174-7, paper, 152 pp.

AELRED OF RIEVAULX—THE WAY OF FRIENDSHIP
M. BASIL PENNINGTON (ed.)
ISBN 1-56548-128-3-0, paper, 168 pp.

BERNARD OF CLAIRVAUX—A LOVER TEACHING THE WAY OF LOVE
M. BASIL PENNINGTON (ed.)
ISBN 1-56548-089-9, 3d printing, paper, 128 pp.

MEDIEVAL WOMEN MYSTICS—Gertrude the Great, Angela of Foligno,
Birgitta of Sweden, Julian of Norwich
ELIZABETH RUTH OBBARD (ed.)
ISBN 1-56548-157-7, 2d printing, paper, 168 pp.

CATHERINE OF SIENA—PASSION FOR THE TRUTH . . .
MARY O'DRISCOLL, O.P. (ed.)
ISBN 1-56548-058-9, 6th printing, paper, 144 pp.

JULIAN OF NORWICH—JOURNEYS INTO JOY
JOHN NELSON (ed.)
ISBN 1-56548-134-8, 2d printing, paper, 184 pp.

THOMAS AQUINAS—THE GIFTS OF THE SPIRIT
BENEDICT M. ASHLEY, O.P. (ed.)
ISBN 1-56548-071-6, 3d printing, paper, 144 pp.

SAINT BENEDICT—A RULE FOR BEGINNERS
JULIAN STEAD, O.S.B. (ed.)
ISBN 1-56548-057-0, 5th printing, paper, 160 pp.

MARTIN LUTHER—FAITH IN CHRIST AND THE GOSPEL
ERIC W. GRITSCH (ed.)
ISBN 1-56548-041-4, 2d printing, paper, 192 pp.

FRANCIS DE SALES—FINDING GOD WHEREVER YOU ARE
JOSEPH F. POWER, O.S.F.S. (ed.)
ISBN 1-56548-074-0, 5th printing, paper, 160 pp.

TEILHARD DE CHARDIN—RECONCILIATION IN CHRIST
JEAN MAALOUF (ed.)
ISBN 1-56548-169-0, paper, 208 pp.

TO ORDER PHONE 1-800-462-5980